TIMES THEY ARE A-CHANGIN'

As Told by a Couple
Happily Married (Most
Days) for 50+ Years

Mary McSwain Steele

& Steven M. Steele

Copyright © 2023 Mary McSwain Steele & Steven M. Steele

Cover Design:
Laura Steele Eckert,
New Creation Photography

All rights reserved.

ISBN-13: 9798865705994

This is Dedicated to the Ones We Love

Mary and I were not quite 20 when we were married in 1971. Two years later, our first child was born. Though we thought ourselves mature and wise, we discovered along the way that we didn't possess the volume and depth of wisdom it would take to raise Joe, Aaron, and Laura.

On this journey of family growth, we realized that the five of us essentially grew up together; we raised each other. We would not have become the parents we are without our children being the wonderful gifts they are.

These three kids of ours, who were so easy and cooperative, so smart, wise, and successful on their own, made us wonder why we should be so blessed. They continued to show good judgment when they chose their life partners. They, along with their spouses, are the treasure of our lives.

So, we dedicate this book to them, knowing all the while that the happy memories and any wisdom that might be found here are due in large part to the kind of children they were and the adults they are today.

Contents

Prologue: We've Only Just Begun

1: Memories May Be Beautiful and Yet… 1
2: I Was Born in a Small Town 5
3: Mammas, Don't Let Your Babies Grow Up to Be Cowboys 12
4: A Change is Gonna Come 17
5: Fly Me to the Moon 23
6: If I Could Save Time in a Bottle 29
7: The First Time Ever I Saw Her Face 33
8: My Eyes Adored You 38
9: Walk Hand in Hand With Me 44
10: Baby's Got Blue Eyes 48
11: How Can I Be Sure? 54
12: Double Your Pleasure, Double Your Fun 60
13: Brown-Eyed Girl 66
14: The Long and Winding Road 72
15: Happy Together 78
16: There's Got to be a Morning After 84
17: You Know It Don't Come Easy 91
18: Just a Man and His Will to Survive 97
19: Breaking Up Is Hard to Do 103
20: Swiftly Fly the Years 109
21: It's NOT Too Late to Turn Back Now 115
22: Come Fly with Me 122
23: The Things We Do for Love 128
24: A Time to Every Purpose Under Heaven 134
25: You Are the Sunshine of Our Lives 141
26: The Sounds of Music 148
27: Shower the People You Love with Love 155
28: Keeps Me Searching for a Heart of Gold 161

29: Before You Go 167
30: I Just Want to Celebrate 173
31: Sweet Home-Away-From-Home Alabama 181
32: We Are the World: Meeting Memusi, Part 1 188
33: We Are the Children: Meeting Memusi, Part 2 195
34: My Grandma, She Wrote Me a Letter 203
35: I'll Have to Say I Love You in a Song 208
36: This One's for You, Mom 214
37: I Am a Rock, I Am an Island 220
38: I've Had the Time of My Life 227
39: I'm Still Standing 233
40: These Are a Few of My Favorite Things 240
41: Hit Me with Your Best Shot 247
42: If I Could Turn Back Time 254
43: But That Was Yesterday, and Yesterday's Gone 260
44: In My Heart, You'll Always Be Forever Young 267
45: Words Get in the Way 273
46: Teach Your Children Well 279
47: Teach Your Grandchildren Well 287
48: We Are Family 293
49: I Guess That's Why They Call It the Blues 301
50: A Change Would Do You Good 306
51: These Are the Best Days of Our Lives 312
Epilogue: Put a Little Love in Your Heart

In Appreciation: We Get by With a Little Help From Our Friends
Authors' Notes: Looks Like We Made It

Prologue: We've Only Just Begun

The question I often get from readers of my first book, *Betty: A Memoir*, is: When is your next book coming out?

Ta-da! Here it is!

I began writing *Betty* at 59, soon after my mother died and before I knew it would be a book. I finished the memoir at age 69.

No one was more surprised than me by the overwhelmingly positive and encouraging responses to Mom's story. She was a single woman in rural Wisconsin, raising three children while working as a nurse. After her children were grown, she traveled to 27 countries on five continents while living and working in the Middle East.

Since publishing *Betty: A Memoir*, I've done several presentations and book signings for libraries, bookstores, book club meetings, and community groups. My husband, Steve, and I have led workshops on "Writing Your Memoir." Regardless of the type of gathering, I usually start my spiel by encouraging "older" people to record their memories for future generations so that those stories won't get lost in history.

Then, I realized, "Hey, wait! I'm one of those older people. I wrote about my mother, but what about my life? And what about my 50+ years with my husband Steve? We could write a book!" (Literally.)

This story is different than *Betty: A Memoir*. For one thing, it's co-authored by Steve.

When we started writing the book, our plan was to explore how the world, the country, and our lives have changed since 1951, the year we were born. (Or not?) We also wanted to explore how our views differ from each other's and how much they are alike.

We even developed a working title (with a little help from Bob Dylan): *The Times They Are A-Changin': A Look Back at the Past Seven Decades as Told by a Couple Happily Married (Most Days) for 50+ Years.*

Then the doubts started rolling in:

But... Our lives aren't as fascinating as Mom's. After all, we didn't spend nine years working in Saudi Arabia and weren't invited to picnics in the desert hosted by Arab sheiks. Steve was a teacher, and I was a journalist-turned-non-profit director in Iowa, both now retired. Why would readers want to read about our "adventures?"

Or... Maybe we're too old to write a book. Can we still remember those events from decades ago? I can barely remember how to tie my shoes. (In my defense, most of my shoes are slip-on these days.)

And... Will anyone want to hear how two Midwest 70-somethings grew up, fell in love, and raised their kids? Do they want to read about our thoughts on religion and politics and child raising? Do they even care about the massive changes we've seen over the years?

Also... What if we embarrass our children and grandchildren? (Scratch that. That will likely happen whether we write a book or not.)

Then we told ourselves: Why not give it a try? What have we got to lose? (Our reputations, our privacy, our sanity… The list goes on.)

We told ourselves the same thing we tell want-to-be memoir writers: Just write one story at a time. One chapter at a time. One page at a time. One sentence… Well, you get the picture.

We envision this book to be written in a "he said/she said" format. The plan is to alternate writing chapters—one from Steve's point of view, followed by my perspective. (I get the last word. As usual.)

The story was first published on Kindle Vella, a newer Amazon Kindle platform. We posted two episodes a week for 25 weeks without photos. The "episodes" on KV are now "chapters" in paperback, hardcover, and e-book formats.

We've also changed the chapter titles, using (and often misusing) song titles that have been popular during our 72 years. We hope you'll read the chapter titles and that they will bring back memories from your earlier days as they did for us. I'll admit that we had trouble getting some of the songs out of our heads. "Earworms," I think they're called, but a pleasant, welcome, nostalgic earworm.

Another of our goals is to test the old adage that two people who have been married 52+ years begin to think alike. Or is it look alike? Either way, we'll analyze those assumptions.

Ultimately, our goal is to write about topics ranging from personal experiences to world events that have occurred in our lifetime. We may discover that, though the times have changed, many things remain the same.

Or not.

Perhaps you've had some of the same experiences, thoughts, and memories discussed in these chapters. They may make you think: "That's exactly how I feel!" Or: "I can relate to that!" Or maybe: "I couldn't disagree more!"

We also hope to encourage others to write their stories. More about that in future chapters.

If we accomplish what we set out to do—if we get you recalling your memories and examining your opinions and attitudes on various topics—maybe even comparing them to your significant others' thoughts. If we motivate you to write **your** story, we will have reached our goals for the book.

We hope that some of our stories will make you laugh, some will warm your heart, and some will help you recall happy times over the course of your life, regardless of how many birthdays you've celebrated.

You may have some questions.

1. **You might be asking what our target audience is.** Our answer: Anyone who was young once and is growing older. You don't have to be 72 to notice the changes around you in technology, fashion, music, education, cars, families, religion, ethics... and pretty much everything.
2. **What is the format?** *Times They Are a-Changin'...* is available in paperback, hardcover, and e-book on Amazon/Kindle. The earlier version on Kindle Vella is still available in a pay-as-you-read format.
3. **What if I want to communicate with the authors?** You can share your thoughts, comments, questions, and critiques with us on our Facebook business page, *Mary McSwain Steele – Author*. There's also email information at the end of this book. We'd love to hear your feedback, and if you'd write a review of

"Times…" and/or "Betty: A Memoir" on Amazon and/or Goodreads, it would be very much appreciated.

And so here we go, looking back, comparing the past to the present, but always hoping to be hopeful about the future.

Our next adventure: writing a book together

TIMES THEY ARE A-CHANGIN'

1
Memories May Be Beautiful and Yet...

"Memory is a way of holding onto the things you love, the things you are, the things you never want to lose."

Implied in this quote is the ability to remember and to relive those experiences from years gone by. Because there are so many memories for all of us, the challenge is to record them somehow before they are lost again in an aging mind.

Incredible experiences and stories are locked up inside every person who walks this earth: joys, sorrows, images, sounds, and smells. So much—*too much*—to be lost.

Here are some of my earliest memories:

I was born one August morning in 1951 by C-section, which suggests that there was either some emergency involved or, as my brothers have suggested, that I was just being overly dramatic at a very early age. As it turns out, Mom had her appendix removed during the procedure, which prompted my wife's suggestion that I would never have been born at all if it had not been for Mom's infected appendix. Humor is intended here. (I think).

My first memory is of being carried on my mother's hip at the country school my five older sisters and brothers attended. Grant Township #4 was one mile east of the farm where I grew up, about 4 miles north of the little town of Sutherland, Iowa. My brothers and sisters walked the mile to school most of the time, depending on the weather.

I remember visiting the school as a toddler, my mother holding me at the front of the classroom next to the blackboard. Everything seemed very large to me. Someone was writing on the board. I liked the sound of chalk on the slate of the board—it gave me goosebumps.

Another special day in my memory is visiting my brother's second-grade classroom. I would have been 3 or 4. By this time, country schools in the area around Sutherland had been consolidated into one big school in town. There must not have been enough room in the school building for every class, so Tom's second-grade class met in the Sutherland Library basement about a block north of the big three-story red-brick school building.

On Visitors' Day at the school, my next-oldest brother, Tom, invited me to be his guest. His teacher was Mrs. Sweeney, and I sat on her lap while she read me a story. Mrs. Sweeney never knew that this early experience made me want to be in school.

The wind is a constant force in Northwest Iowa, blowing and pushing anything not fastened down. It seems like the wind blows every day the year around. A small door on our barn sometimes would not get latched. On a breezy day, it would bang open and blow shut all day. That door banging, combined with the yellowish angle of the afternoon sun during the school year, was a desolate sound and a lonely time of day for me.

It always made me wish that my brothers and sisters would get home from school. Irritating as they could sometimes be, I missed them when they were gone. I would sit in the bay window on the south side of the house, watching for the kids. That was also where Mom kept most of her houseplants, and I associated the tart odor of the geraniums with loneliness.

After the country schools had combined to form the Sutherland Consolidated School, my siblings would be picked up early in the morning and delivered home by a short, yellow school bus. Tim and Tom were off first, running with coats half on, half off. Virginia and Sue, the oldest of six kids, would follow, carrying a stack of books. Phil, the oldest of us four boys, would be last.

Phil was the beast of burden for the girls. I think they had learned how to take advantage of his good nature. He would have his books, Virginia's French horn, Sue's trombone, and his trumpet. I have often wondered if they ever argued about these arrangements or if Phil was just nice.

By the time I was old enough to attend school myself, I felt I was already grown up. Reading the newspaper appeared to be a very mature thing to do, so I would hold the paper up in front of me like my dad and stare at the words, even though I couldn't read them yet. Pretending to read the paper made me want to understand the words.

At times, I wanted to sound like an adult, so I would make up a story and speak it out loud as if I were reading to someone.

I would even lower my voice, so I sounded older.

I loved reading the "funnies," as we called the comics section, and I truly enjoyed studying them. I liked the artistry of even simple drawings. I wondered, "How do they know how to do that? How does the artist know what Blondie looks like?" Beetle Baily, Blondie, and Dick Tracey were my favorites. The characters were an encouragement for me to read and discover their stories.

It seems strange sometimes how the smallest of events change our lives. Who would have known this farm boy would become an educator, teaching science for 38 years? (As to why I chose to teach science, I'll be covering that in a later episode.)

These memories are of an age where every day brought something new: a discovery, an invention, a new style. Looking back at those growing-up years, I realize we were the luckiest kids in the world.

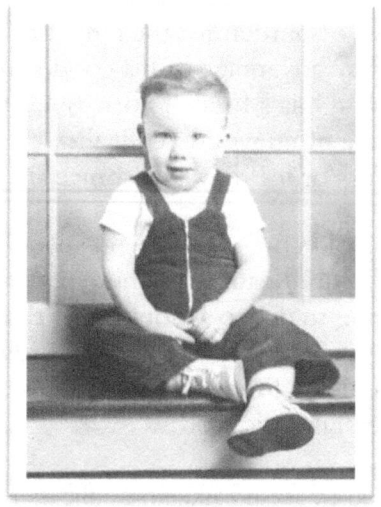

This is me at about 2 years old.

2
I Was Born in a Small Town

I was born early on Sunday morning, July 29, 1951. Truman was president, Joe DiMaggio retired from baseball, gas was 19 cents a gallon, and television's popularity grew with the first broadcast of color TV.

My parents worked at the Viroqua Hospital in southwest Wisconsin—my dad was a lab technician, and my mom was a nurse. Our family lived 10 miles south of Viroqua in the small village of Readstown, population 469, along the Kickapoo River.

When Mom finished her shift on the evening of July 28, the other nurses convinced her to stay overnight at the hospital instead of driving home. They were concerned that if she went home and the Kickapoo flooded over the bridge linking Viroqua and Readstown as predicted, she wouldn't be able to return to the hospital if she went into labor.

As it turned out, Mom made a good decision when she reluctantly agreed to spend the night at the hospital. Over eight inches of rain fell during the last week of July, and floodwaters tore through the Kickapoo Valley. Nearby, Gays Mills was submerged five feet deep in water, and buildings floated away from the tiny town of Boaz.

And so, conveniently, Mom was already at the hospital when she had me, her second child. My sister Susan was born just 21 months earlier, and less than two years after my birth, my brother Michael was born. Legend has it that when Susan and I heard squeaking noises from the blanketed bundle in Mom's arms, we thought our parents had brought a puppy home for us. We were disappointed to learn that the swaddled bundle was a baby brother instead.

When our family moved to Jensen Beach, FL, Mike was only a year old. I'm not sure why my parents chose Florida as their new residence. Mom was born and raised in Readstown, and my dad grew up in Paris, TN.

I was only about three years old, so my earliest memories are of only a few isolated events during our two years in Florida.

I remember being excited when my dad brought home a baby alligator from the hospital where he worked. I'm not sure how he happened to be in possession of a baby alligator, but I think one of his co-workers at the hospital gave it to him. We named the alligator Oscar. He was just a few inches long when my dad brought him home to us.

Unfortunately, Oscar got too big to keep. I'm not sure what constitutes "too big" for a pet alligator in an apartment with three preschoolers, but I think I remember that our pet was flushed down the toilet. Susan remembers the loss of Oscar differently. She says he was about two feet long when our dad released him into a swamp at the end of our street. Neither seems like an ideal way to dispose of a pet alligator.

I also have flashes of memory of walking across the beautiful grounds of the luxurious Fontainebleau Hotel in Miami Beach to see the magnificent fountain in front of the lobby. Our parents gave each of us kids a penny and told us we could make a wish and toss it into the fountain. They said it would come true if we didn't tell anyone what we wished.

I clearly remember wishing that someday I would meet a really nice man, marry him, and live happily ever after. Susan kept bugging me to tell her what I had wished for, but I didn't share it with anyone. My wish came true 16 years later when I married "a really nice man."

Sadly, my father had an alcohol problem and maybe other health or emotional issues I'm unaware of. Even at a very young age, I knew that our financial situation was a tense topic, so one day, Susan and I decided to do our part to help with the family's money problems. I remember the two of us sitting at a small kids' table with raw potatoes and two plastic knives. We peeled the potatoes and cut them into little tooth-shaped pieces.

When Mom asked what we were doing, we proudly explained that we were going to put the small white potato pieces under our pillows for the Tooth Fairy. We had left our lost teeth under our pillows before, and coins had appeared magically the next day. We would give the money raised from our little fundraiser to our parents to pay bills.

My mom patiently explained to us that it would be wrong to try to fool the Tooth Fairy, and we were disappointed when she made us throw away the potato pieces (which had started to turn brown). It was perhaps our first lesson in finance ethics.

When Mom decided we would be better off without our dad, she took her three young children home to Readstown on a Greyhound bus. It is a 1,500-mile trip that takes 22 hours by car. I don't know how many hours we were on the bus or how many layovers we had, but Susan remembers having motion sickness and throwing up most of the trip.

Me, Mike, and Susan catch up on our reading, though I appear to be daydreaming instead of reading.

We moved into Mom's parents' two-story, three-bedroom house in Readstown for two or three years. At the time, her dad's bachelor brother, Charlie, lived with Grandma and Grandad Rosson and occupied an upstairs bedroom. Charlie seldom talked, but I snuck into his room when he was gone once. I was amazed to see bookshelves on nearly every wall, all filled with paperbacks, most of which were Zane Grey books.

Mom got her job back at the Viroqua hospital and lived frugally, saving every penny she could. We ate a lot of big bologna sandwiches, and finally, she was able to buy a new trailer home for our family.

Despite my parents' rocky marriage, the sudden move from Florida to Wisconsin, and the absence of a father, I had a relatively happy childhood. As is the case in most small towns, all the kids knew each other. We played games in our adjoining backyards until dark: Red Rover, Starlight, Star Bright, Hide and Seek, and Kick-the-Can.

On the rare occasions when there weren't a bunch of neighborhood kids around, we played hopscotch or marbles on the sidewalk with our siblings. We rode our bikes through the streets all over town. There were no bike trails back then, but there wasn't much traffic for our parents to worry about. One of our favorite biking destinations was the city cemetery, an interesting place to visit. We would stop and examine the headstones, taking special interest in the ones with photos, birth and death dates in the 1800s, and those with names etched into them that were the same as ours.

Readstown kids had a special place of their own that we called Tree Town, which was halfway up the hill near our house. There, along what we called the "Indian Path" (more likely a cow path), we built rustic tree houses from scraps of boards and rusty nails, using old tools we found in our garages.

We spent hours each summer day at our magical place in the woods, always remodeling or building additions to our houses in the branches. When the leaves started to fall in late summer, we could see all of the village of Readstown from our perches in the trees.

In the winter, we would sled down the hill in the back of the new elementary school building. More than once, we hauled a friend home on a toboggan after crashing on the icy slope, often sporting a goose egg on his or her head. Readstown also had a make-shift ice rink, created when the volunteer firemen flooded an empty field next to the tobacco warehouse. Most of us got to be pretty good skaters at a young age.

(Does anyone remember when kids' entertainment didn't require a device, buying a new video game, or downloading an app? I kind of miss those days.)

I liked school, although I wasn't the best student in my grade school classes of around 20 kids. That might be because when we were supposed to be working on an assignment, I sometimes sneaked a library book out of my desk drawer and read it on my lap instead of doing homework. I remember the line "Mary spends too much time daydreaming" appearing in the comments section of several of my report cards.

I was more interested in reading and writing than math and science. (Just ask my chemistry teacher, Mr. Kellogg. He gave me my first and only "D," which was a gift.) Years later, I would choose journalism as my college major.

I still keep in touch with many of my grade school and high school friends and a few special teachers. Although I haven't lived in Wisconsin for more than 50 years, I return to Readstown as often as possible. Steve has also developed a love of the beauty of rural Wisconsin and enjoys the trip as much as I do. We drive south through the hills and valleys along Highway 14, across the bridge over the Kickapoo River, and then take a left turn into town.

I immediately see the little white church where Steve and I were married. My grandparents' house still stands on Front Street, though they've been gone for several decades. At the end of Back Street is the hill where we went sledding. I look up at the tree-covered hills and remember where my friends and I spent long summer days. I wonder if any Readstown kids today have their own version of Tree Town.

As we drive through the tree-covered rolling hills, I have a warm feeling of contentment and security. I'm home again.

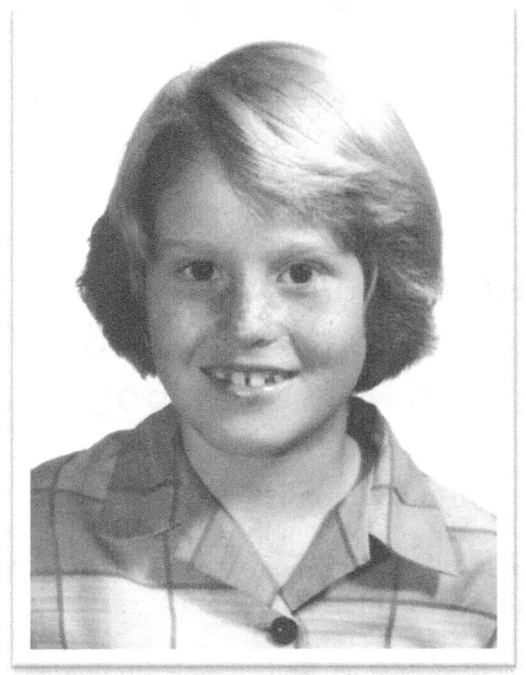

Me at eight years old. I never wore braces (too expensive!), but fortunately, the gaps disappeared when I got more teeth.

3
Mammas, Don't Let Your Babies Grow Up to Be Cowboys

I was elated when I learned we would finally be getting a television. As the youngest in the family by several years, nobody really tells you anything—except what to do and, "Mind your own business!"

Hearing the news that we were getting our own television made me think we were suddenly rich. At seven years old in 1958, I hadn't considered value systems yet.

The first TV I ever saw was at the home of church friends. It sat in the corner of their dark living room and had a softly lighted border around the screen—the effect was called halo lights. It was magic, like someone had put my imagination on a screen.

In my first TV viewing, I saw images of bombs being dropped on a city with huge explosions and fire consuming buildings. The television was an incredible device that could conjure up those magic images. I was an instant TV addict.

I saw my first western show on another friend's television, watching intently as cowboys herded cattle and drove them to market. On the long ride home from school, the bus would pass farm pastures with cattle grazing. As I watched, my mind had me on a horse chasing strays and roping cattle at roundup for branding, usually with another cowboy I named "Dusty."

The daily one-hour bus trip home from school was agonizingly long but exciting for this second grader. I wondered if **this** would be the day our television arrived from Montgomery Ward. The images I saw on my friends' TVs kept running repeatedly in my mind.

The day finally came. Our new TV was a Sylvania (such an exotic name!) from Montgomery Ward. That's where we seemed to get most of our new things; everything else came from the thrift store in town. It was black and white, of course. I wouldn't see a color TV for several years.

The air was electric with excitement at our farm, but we had to do the chores before the TV would be installed. All of us kids worked on completing our jobs without complaining—we usually did our share of bellyaching, but out of my parent's hearing range.

When the chores were finished, Dad climbed up on the roof in the near dark to install the antenna and point it southwest toward Sioux City. Then he ran the flat brown antenna wire through brackets screwed into the roof and down the side of the house and then through the window closest to the corner of the living room where our new TV was sitting.

Dad was as excited as we were. He came down from the roof, carefully hooked up the TV, proudly turned it on, and... it didn't work! The screen looked like a blizzard. Not even a hint of a picture.

My dad climbed back onto the roof to make sure the antenna was pointed toward Sioux City, and still, there was nothing on the screen but snow. We all waited quietly, expecting Dad to lose his temper, but he kept it together, for which everyone was relieved.

The faulty television was returned to Montgomery Ward and exchanged for a new one. The replacement television worked, at least as well as it could. The distance from Sioux City was too great and challenged the technology of the time. The weather on any given day could bounce the signals around, and we couldn't get anything but the faintest snowy picture that ghosted in and out.

But it was enough to fuel a seven-year-old's imagination. Through the variety and creativity of television, I gained a new and faithful companion. My young brain found it difficult to separate fiction from reality. It had me under its spell.

Right after getting off the school bus in the afternoon, I liked to watch a local show, "The Canyon Kid," which featured cartoons and prizes. "Rocky the Flying Squirrel" and "Yogi, the Bear" were also two of my favorites. I considered that time slot, right after getting off the bus, to be mine. Once, when it was time to do chores, and I didn't respond to Mom's voice, she came in and snapped off the TV.

I was upset and threw a crying tantrum in front of my mom. I'll never know what made me think this was a good idea. The only effect this had on her, other than to realize I had become an exceptionally spoiled youngest child, was that I needed special attention. I had never thrown a fit like that, and it did not work with my mom. Not at all.

One of my favorite TV characters was Zorro, as evidenced by the t-shirt I wore proudly. (Mom had forgotten it was picture day.)

The fantasy of TV westerns became a part of how I played with my next-oldest brother, Tom. We liked to act and talk like the bad guys on "Two Gun Playhouse." Once, I was hiding just around the corner of a farm building when Tom came by, and I hit him in the head with a rock, like the cowboys on TV. Just knock a guy unconscious with whatever you have handy. How could that really hurt?

Fortunately, I didn't hit him hard enough to knock him out, but made his scalp bleed. I got to thinking: Could it be that those people don't really hit each other when they make those shows? It was the first time I wondered about the authenticity of what I saw on TV.

A turning point occurred when I was using our single-shot BB gun to hunt tin cans, fence posts, and such. As I walked by the house, hunting for "bad guys," Tom stood at the window of my parent's bedroom. He made a face and pointed his finger at me like a pistol. Not thinking, I shot at him with the BB gun. Fortunately, the window only cracked. I'm embarrassed to say that I lied to my parents to avoid punishment.

I was not the only victim of the influence of television. Through it, the "world" came into our very conservative home. When a commercial came on advertising cigarettes or beer, my sisters, voluntarily or by order of the parents, turned down the sound and covered the TV screen with their skirts.

The attempt at censorship didn't last long, though. I think the girls got tired of the task, and we boys thought the Hamm's Beer commercials with the bear were hilarious.

4
A Change is Gonna Come

Ah, the '60s. Peace and love. Flower children. Tie-dyed T-shirts, sandals, and bell bottoms. Hula hoops. The Beatles, Rock 'n' Roll. First Super Bowl. Scientific breakthroughs: big events like astronauts walking on the moon. Less significant but more relatable: advances like color TV, stereo sound, 8-track tapes, and the first practical use of computers.

The 1960s also brought a move toward inclusiveness: the Civil Rights Movement, the election of the first Irish Catholic president, the free speech movement, and women's lib. Conversely, the '60s were also a time of divisiveness: the War in Vietnam, the Bay of Pigs, the Cuban Missile Crisis, and the assassination of JFK, MLK and Bobby Kennedy.

Besides political changes on the national level, there were shifts in societal and cultural life on a more personal level. Young people began to question the values of the previous generation. Long-held beliefs about family, religion, and morality were challenged, often through public protests, which sometimes turned violent. Draft cards were burned. As were bras.

Are you impressed with my knowledge of the '60s? And perhaps, awed by my ability to remember events from 60+ years ago in such great detail? Don't be. I googled to get those facts with a few keystrokes and minimal effort.

Remember when researching for a homework assignment meant spending hours looking through a card catalog and dozens of library books to get info that Google can get in seconds? Those days are gone.

But I digress. I do remember these important events, but none of the specific dates or details. That could be because I became a teenager in 1964 and had more important things on my mind. Like my hair and my clothes, hiding my freckles with my first attempts at makeup, listening to all the latest hits on WLS Radio, and talking on the phone for hours with girlfriends (but only when my mom was at work or she would have put a stop to that nonsense).

Oh, and boys. I had begun to take an interest in the opposite sex. Nothing serious. I wasn't "boy crazy." Quite the opposite—I was shy, quiet, seriously lacking in self-confidence, and not at all flirty.

My first boyfriends, if you can call them that, were boys I met at church camp. Those relationships lasted about as long as camp—one week. Sometimes, they stretched out to a month or two through letter writing (tedious and time-consuming) and rare long-distance phone calls (expensive). There was no social media, no texting, and no Facetime chats back in the '60s.

I do remember one cute guy, Jeff, who sent me a bobblehead

doll from the World's Fair in New York City. I wonder where he is and what he's doing now. It didn't take long before the relationship faded away.

That changed when I was 15 and a freshman in high school. Our church hired a new minister, and he and his family (which included five sons) moved to Readstown. I began dating one of the boys in the fall of 1966.

It was my first "real" boy/girl relationship. It lasted about three years—for me, anyway. The relationship was over for him not long after he went off to college in the fall of 1967. I still had three years left of high school, dooming any chances of the forever relationship with the preacher's son I had daydreamed about.

My heart was broken. Or maybe more accurately, at 16 years old, it *felt* like I had a broken heart. (Looking back, I think it was probably just a sprain.)

Although it was a painful new experience, the breakup didn't keep me from enjoying my remaining high school years. Kickapoo High School was a small, consolidated school in southwest Wisconsin where everyone knew everyone. We had great teachers, some who were not much older than their students.

Athletics were a big part of KHS, but most schools in our conference only offered athletic opportunities to boys. That seems strange now, in these days of Title IX, which makes it illegal to discriminate on the basis of gender. But we thought nothing of it then. Girls (but not guys) could try out for cheerleading for the boys' sports. Those of us who didn't make the varsity cheering squad or the JV squad were happy to support our teams from the bleachers.

As a junior, I was selected by teachers and student council

members in 1968 to represent KHS as a foreign exchange student. I was fortunate to be placed with a warm and loving family in Rio de Janeiro, Brazil. The Tabet family seemed so excited to host this American girl who knew only a few words of Portuguese. Luckily, they spoke English. The whole family did everything possible to make me feel welcome, including taking me to a "futbol" game starring the legendary soccer player Pele'.

It was an incredible experience that made a lasting impression on me. Over the past 50+ years, I have kept in touch with my Brazilian family and have visited them twice, once in Brazil and once in Canada.

My high school senior picture, 1969

I was happy and relieved when my high school graduation day finally arrived. My classmates, the KHS Class of '69, were extremely close. I knew I would miss my high school friends, but I was ready to move on to college. It wasn't so much that I wanted to find new challenges, get an education and a job, or even meet new friends. Mostly, I just wanted to be on my own.

My mom, who raised three children alone and worked full-time as a nurse, was not a June Cleaver type of mother. She could sometimes be critical, controlling, and difficult to live with. Mom was never physically abusive, and I know she wanted only the best for us, but I was looking forward to a less restrictive environment.

I chose a small, conservative Christian college in Nebraska, partly because my sister Susan and several friends from church were also going there. In retrospect, I see the irony of wanting to get out from under my mother's overbearing personality and then choosing to go to a college with many rules.

The school had a strictly enforced dress code. Girls were required to wear dresses or skirts to classes—no pants or jeans. The skirts had to be at least knee length. If faculty members thought a dress was too short, they'd have the girl get down on her knees to see if the hem touched the floor. If it didn't, she would have to return to the dorm and change clothes. There were rules for the guys, too. Male students' hair had to be clipped short—it couldn't touch their collars, and they couldn't wear blue jeans to classes.

Pool and card playing were forbidden. Attendance at weekly chapel services was required. And, as you might expect, no alcohol or tobacco use was allowed—on or off campus. Breaking the rules could, and sometimes did, result in students being expelled.

Despite all the rules, some of which I thought were arbitrary and had no basis in scripture, I was thrilled with my new environment. I felt freer than I'd ever been in my life. Living in the dorm was an adventure. I made friends from all over the country, and many of us still keep in touch largely due to social media.

I've never regretted my college choice for many reasons, but mostly because I met my husband-to-be at that small Christian college.

But that's for another chapter.

These Kickapoo High School grads, including my sister, Susan, all went to the same small college in 1969.

5
Fly Me to the Moon

We choose to go to the moon in this decade and do the other things, not because they are easy, but because they are hard.

~ John F. Kennedy, September 12, 1962

"Now that's strange," I thought when I first heard JFK's quote. While growing up on the farm, this Iowa boy always looked for ways to make life easier. Though foreign, the "doing things because they are hard" concept stayed with me and challenged me. But more about that later.

While a student in the upper elementary grades during the '50s, I discovered I liked science a great deal. And why not? Growing up on the farm is all science: crops, weather, streams, pets, animals, reproduction, sweat, sounds, and smells. I enjoyed reading and thinking about scientific things.

TIMES THEY ARE A-CHANGIN'

I used to stand at the big sink in the mud room and experiment with water balloons, ink, bleach, and other stuff. I was a theory guy, a big picture guy, and a science fiction guy, which is simply one way of saying I was a daydreamer.

Our house was not air-conditioned, and no one I knew had air conditioning in their home either. Sometimes on summer nights, when it was hot and no air was moving, my brothers and I would grab the covers off the bed, take them outside to the front yard, and sleep under the brilliant stars.

Not a single farm had security lights that stayed on all night as they do now. Our yard light was switched off at the end of the day after chores were done. When the sky was clear, we were overwhelmed by the dark and the amazing beauty of the stars. Amidst it all, I saw the first human-made satellite moving silently across the sky.

My brothers told me it was Sputnik, first launched in 1957. Later, I came to understand that Sputnik was a threat to Americans. It was launched by the Soviet Union. That the Russians could launch a tiny satellite into Earth's orbit meant they had better rocket technology to launch whatever they wanted.

Attempts by the United States to launch a satellite had blown up on the launch pad, and many citizens were nervous. My brothers made fun of Sputnik by taking a potato, poking toothpicks in it, and calling it "Spudnik." It didn't take much to entertain us back then.

In January 1958, the U.S. would finally put Explorer I into orbit. By this time, I had sadly come to understand the meaning of this space race. It was more about military capability and superiority than it was about a peaceful, amazing kind of science. In those beautiful moments under the stars, I felt the sky become tainted with danger.

The '60s opened in a whirl of newness. My hometown, Sutherland, had joined with two other small towns, Calumet and Gaza, to become the Sutherland Community School District. This was viewed with some excitement because Calumet had won the Class B Iowa Boys State Basketball Championship in the Spring of '59. A championship in 1960 was an exciting possibility for the newly created school system.

Potential championship aside, there were also the politics of the playground to contend with. Calumet and Sutherland had some previously hotly contested basketball games in the past and were strong rivals. And there was also the jealousy of their success that created tension.

The big question to consider in the first days of school was whether we were supposed to like these new kids since they beat us in basketball. The first recess was all about deep-seated school rivalry. "We could beat you guys at football ... ha, ha!" (It was not a very intelligent comment since Calumet didn't have a football team). That chant lasted about a day. Then we discovered they were nice kids, and we began to have a great time together.

Some other important items of note:

In 1959, Alaska and Hawaii were added as the 49th and 50th states, and along with the change in our country came the change to our flag. I didn't know how they would work two more stars into the flag and make it look balanced and not overcrowded. But somehow, they managed and maybe taught a good lesson at the same time. Everyone, like the stars on the flag, can just "move over" a little to reach the goal.

In November 1960, John F. Kennedy was elected as the new president of the United States. Though there was political concern in my family about him personally because he was Catholic and a Democrat, I found him to be wise and strong.

"Ask not," he said (a strange way to structure a statement, I thought) "what your country can do for you. Ask what you can do for your country." That's imperative if we are to survive as a united and free country in a combative world.

JFK wanted to go into space, the new frontier. I liked that about him. Alan Shepherd was launched into space for a few minutes in May 1961. John Glenn launched and orbited the earth three times in February 1962. For me, those were such special moments.

Although I loved science, I preferred listening to the launches over the school's intercom (advanced technology in the 1960s!) rather than studying science from a book.

Along with those moments of success was the tension of the space race. Though the Soviets were first, I did feel more secure knowing we could do those things, too—and for the "right reasons," of course.

Later in 1962, world politics took center stage. I had a crush on one of the girls in my class (actually, any girl in my class), and I was distracted from most world events, too busy being a boy. But I'd heard enough of the news to admire the strength of our president standing up to the Soviets when we discovered them building missile bases in Cuba.

The Soviet Missile Crisis is thought to have taken the world to the brink of nuclear war in October of that year. I watched news footage of the chilling physical confrontation with Russian ships carrying nuclear missiles to Cuba. We blocked their ships, and they turned back. The world likely avoided a war in that moment.

Fly Me to the Moon

In 7th grade, the announcement that President Kennedy had been shot in Dallas on November 22, 1963, made me feel as if the world would end and that there would be war in our country. I felt like crying, but I didn't want to look weak for all those girls I had crushes on. I walked to the bus numbly and rode the shuttle bus to Sutherland from Calumet in complete silence.

I was lucky that day to have youth choir practice at our church, which was led by my sister, Sue. I don't remember what she said—some words of reassurance, as I recall. She said a prayer for us and over us. And then, we sang our Thanksgiving special song for Sunday. It was the best therapy.

In 1968, Dion recorded a song lamenting the loss of courageous men, "Abraham, Martin, and John." Martin Luther King had just been killed in April of that year. It was a sad song about humans' inhumanity in the face of good.

"He freed a lot of people, but it seems the good; they die young. I looked around, and they were gone," was repeated in each verse. It seemed there was so much heaviness in the '60s—from the struggle for Civil Rights to Vietnam.

Kennedy was right. July 20, 1969, marked the first human step on the Moon. "One small step for man, one giant leap for mankind." It was a foreshadowing of what lay ahead of me.

I would be leaving for college three weeks later. Being out on my own (well, sort of) proved to be a world that this farm boy had not yet dreamed of, but it would turn out to be exciting and challenging.

JFK's words came back to me: "...We do the other things, not because they are easy, but because they are hard."

The cover of the July 25, 1969 issue of Time Magazine depicts Neil Armstrong planting a flag on the moon.

6
If I Could Save Time in a Bottle

Looking back over the past seven decades, I realize now that there were more changes in my life beginning in late 1969 and throughout the '70s than at any other time period before or after. In just ten years, I left home, went to college, got engaged and married, had three children, lived in three different states, and was hired for my first job as a newspaper journalist. Those years were also paradoxical: joyful, stressful, rewarding, challenging, stimulating, and tedious.

My first life-changing event was in 1969 when I chose a college; another was years later when I finally decided on a career. Growing up in the '60s, girls weren't expected to go to college. But if they did, they had basically three choices for areas of study: education, office administration (secretary), or nursing. None of those careers interested me, although I briefly considered being a beautician as a teenager. My mom nixed that career choice, telling me, "You don't want to stand on your feet all day cutting and curling someone's hair!" Obviously, it was something she didn't want to do, and, put like that, it didn't seem like such a glamorous job to me either.

I did briefly consider studying to be an elementary school teacher. That would have been a mistake since, later in life, I would find out that the cuteness of young children can wear off quickly—unless they're your own. More importantly, I didn't think I had the patience and stamina to be around 20 to 30 little kids every day, even with summers off.

Some of my classmates went to college to find a husband, or, as it was referred to in the '60s, to get their MRS degrees. Truthfully, in addition to getting away from home, I chose a small conservative college two states away in the hope of finding the perfect husband.

As with my original career choice, my mom wasn't happy with my college choice. She would have preferred I go to a public school with more options for areas of study. She valued her nurse's training, and it was important to her that each of her children get a good education. Mom had raised three kids as a single parent working full time, and she lived frugally to save enough to pay for her children's college education.

But my choice at the Christian college turned out to be one of the best decisions I've made for several reasons, especially because that's where I met my future husband, Steve.

However, I wasn't impressed the first time I saw him. I was standing in line with friends outside the registrar's office, waiting to sign up for classes (there was no such thing as online registration in the 1960s). I saw a guy standing in the line behind me with bright red hair and a light green shirt that looked too small for him (to show off his football and

If I Could Save Time in a Bottle

weight-lifting physique, I guessed).

He appeared to be going up and down the hall where the line was formed, counting ceiling tiles. Weird. I would find out much later there was a reason for his peculiar behavior, but I'll let him tell you about that.

Although shy and quiet, Steve worked up the courage to ask me to go with him to Wednesday night chapel for our first date. I wasn't all that interested in this bashful, red-haired Iowa farm boy until we stood to sing a hymn during the service. That's when I heard this beautiful voice and realized it was coming from him.

Steve may have lacked confidence with girls, but he sang with the self-assurance and talent of a professional vocalist. I joke, "I dated Steve for his voice—his voice and his money—but it turned out he didn't have any money, so I guess it was really just the voice thing."

Of course, there were other, more significant reasons for choosing Steve. He is the kindest, most loving, and most patient person I've ever met. But it was the way he sang that first hooked me.

After we'd dated a few times, we had a heart-to-heart discussion about our relationship. I told him I didn't want to get tied down to one guy as a freshman in college, and he agreed.

But I immediately regretted my decision to play the field when I saw him with another girl at chapel the following week. My friends in the dorm suggested I invite Steve to the upcoming Sadie Hawkins event before his new "girlfriend" had a chance to invite him first.

The rest is history, as they say.

TIMES THEY ARE A-CHANGIN'

Our first photos together, taken in a photo booth in 1970

7

The First Time Ever I Saw Her Face

It wasn't until the summer after graduating from high school that I decided to attend a small Christian college in Norfolk, Nebraska. I was uncertain and felt threatened at the prospect of leaving home.

It's not that I didn't want to be independent; I simply felt unprepared to do so. My fear was so real that I gathered the nerve to start a conversation with Dad about the possibility of staying home on the farm, working with him, and, at some point, renting land to get started farming on my own.

Consider the lack of logic in that train of thought. Here was a young man who wanted to leave home and go his own direction in life, and yet he asked to partner with his father because it felt more secure. It sounded like the beginning of the parable of the lost son when he talks to his father about his future. (Except I wasn't asking Dad for my inheritance to spend on wild living.)

Fathers of that era, the 1960s, were generally not warm, touchy-feely guys. This was the first and only real heart-to-heart conversation I'd ever initiated with my dad. His advice was short and to the point, forever changing my life.

"The price of land is $400 an acre," he told me. "The price of corn is $1.00 per bushel. You couldn't make enough to pay interest or rent land at those prices."

Notice his use of the pronoun "you" and not "we." Then Dad said, "You should just go on to college."

And with that, the conversation was over. It surprised me a little. I was his youngest son, and I thought he might need help with the farm operation since he was getting older. I guess Dad wasn't feeling "older" at 52, and my foster brother Keith would still be home for another year.

I didn't bother to verify Dad's statement that farming was not profitable because he always had the final word. There was no point in discussing it further. Later in life, I would understand that he made that decision for me because he knew I didn't have the desire or the will to be a farmer.

As another wise person told me later, "You don't **think** like a farmer."

He was right. To me, the excrement on the end of the pitchfork was not money, it was poop, and it didn't "smell like money," it smelled like poop. As much as I appreciated the strength building of body and mind that resulted from all the farm work—the shoveling, baling, and digging post holes—it was still poop.

The First Time Ever I Saw Her Face

Dad was right, too, and he was wise to tell me to go to college instead of farm. He knew, without asking, that moving on was what I wanted, even needed. Though I loved being on the farm, I didn't love farming.

The small college I chose was familiar and safe for me. All but one of my siblings had attended there. The school had a faith connection with my family and our church. And there was an additional factor: I had received an athletic scholarship at the junior college in the same town.

That's how I came to find myself in the hallway outside the college business office in September of 1969. That fall was dry; the trees were starting to turn golden, and the cicadas were singing their lonely, buzzing song. The hit tune from the Young Rascals, "How Can I Be Sure," was a favorite of mine that kept going through my mind. It had been a kind of security blanket since being dumped by my girlfriend four months earlier.

While waiting in line to register for classes with some new friends, I was thinking about what classes I had to take, wondering if I had options. I became bored and started counting the holes in the acoustic tiles in the hallway's ceiling. I was making a small production of the process and got laughs from the guys.

Besides relieving my boredom, the real reason for this was to get attention in general, specifically, the attention of a small group of girls standing some distance away in the corner of the dining hall. Who wouldn't be impressed by a college freshman farm kid who could count, add, and multiply?

Clearly, I was not a master of simple social skills like personal introductions and enlightened conversation. What should be so simple and natural was still far beyond my reach. Getting attention in some harmless and perhaps humorous way was my attempt at beginning a conversation with the girls. I don't think they even noticed me.

I was focused especially on a young woman with long red hair who radiated elegance and confidence. The idea that any of the group would be interested in what I was doing would be a stretch and, for sure, not the beautiful redhead with the great tan.

One of the first things I noticed about Mary was her golden tan.

She was certainly out of my league. The risk of rejection was too strong to contemplate, so I half-heartedly finished my counting project, waited my turn to register for the fall semester, and wondered if she would be in any of my classes.

Imagine my surprise when, two weeks later, one of the redhead's friends, Lynn, stopped me in the hall. I knew her a little because we were in choir and some of the same classes together, plus she was dating a friend. She told me there was someone special who wanted to meet me.

"Come over to the front porch of the girl's dorm tonight, and I will introduce you," she said.

The First Time Ever I Saw Her Face

The promise of an introduction was a huge incentive for me as it cut the risk of beginning a conversation by half. I was still anxious but excited at the same time. I was amazed to find out it was the beautiful and distant redhead with the tan who was interested in meeting me! I felt as if I were standing in the headlights of an oncoming truck, with deer eyes and all.

I tried to appear cool and calm, if not confident, as I was introduced to Mary McSwain from the exotic-sounding state of Wisconsin. After saying, "Hello, nice to meet you" (I did have enough wits about me to remember to smile), we stood beside each other, not saying a word, as we watched the others make plans for a get-acquainted roller-skating party.

My heart was pounding, and I thought I would pass out. How could I, an 18-year-old farm boy, not melt in the gaze of that young, brown-eyed woman? What was there about me that she would be interested in? How could I measure up to this beauty? Silently, I panicked, my brain short-circuiting.

Is that any way to start a relationship? One this tenuous can't last... Or can it?

8
My Eyes Adored You

When I was 12, Mom and Dad gave me a telescope for Christmas. It was a small, simple set of convex lenses in a metal casing. The user held it up to one eye and focused by moving the last section in or out, like a sailor high in the crow's nest of a pirate ship looking for another ship to pillage.

By any scientific standard, it was a poor-quality instrument. The image produced was slightly fuzzy at the edges, with hints of different colors of the spectrum smudged in. But I thought it was beautiful, and no one I knew had one. I was entranced when I looked through my new telescope at the moon.

I couldn't believe how brightly the moon reflected light and how many crater scars and mountains there were on the surface of that quickly moving ball. Keeping the moon in view was a confusing task. The lenses turned the image upside down and didn't move in the direction I knew it should be traveling.

Six years later, the little telescope would help me find my soulmate. What does an inferior-quality telescope have to do with finding my best friend and partner, you might ask? Let me explain.

After being introduced in the fall of '69, Mary McSwain and I learned that we had much in common. We had already discovered that neither of us was very outgoing. We both came from small towns and had similar high school social experiences. Though she seemed exotic to me when I first saw her, she was genuinely down-to-earth, quietly self-confident yet humble, and didn't think too highly of herself.

We also came from the same socio-economic level—in other words, neither of us had much money. After getting to know her, I worked up the nerve to ask her to go out with me.

For our first date, we attended Wednesday night chapel together. It may not sound exciting, but it was considered a big step toward announcing a possible relationship. After the service, I borrowed my brother's car (I was surprised he agreed to loan it to me) and took Mary to "Mary's Café," a popular spot for college kids on the east side of town.

The outfit Mary wore on that first date quickly became my favorite—a red sweater beneath a scoop-neck plaid jumper that her mom had made. Wow! I was mesmerized! I don't even remember what we talked about (you may recall that I had serious brain paralysis around her), but I managed to get through the evening.

My brother's car was a '63 Ford Fairlane hardtop with a high-performance 289 engine and a four-on-the-floor transmission. Mary sat right next to me in the middle of the front seat (there was no seat belt law at the time), and I drove carefully and smoothly, though I might have "accidentally" bumped her knee while shifting gears. I didn't show off, and I safely dropped Mary off at her dorm after our date. I hoped she would be impressed with my driving if not my charm.

Our first date, at Mary's Café (and Mobile station), was the start of 52 years together.

During the next few days, we had some casual conversations during short walks in which we both expressed our desire "not to get tied down." Instead, we agreed we should both be free to meet and get to know "other people."

Or at least, that's what I thought we had agreed to. Mary wore a brown suede leather jacket as we walked around the block on a misty, foggy evening. The scent of the leather mixed with her perfume simply took over my senses, and I would have agreed to anything, having heard nothing.

Based on Mary's earlier statement, "I don't want to get tied down," and the fact that I had gained a bit of confidence in this new frontier of college life, I decided to ask another young woman to chapel the following week. As it turned out, I didn't understand this new frontier at all.

When it became known I was going out with another girl, I was shunned in the hallways by Mary's friends. It was a cool and very quiet existence. While I was walking to class a few days later, wondering what I had done wrong, a car stopped beside me. Mary was in the back seat and one of her friends, Lynn, was in the passenger seat. Lynn asked if she could borrow my watch.

"Mary has a job interview, and she needs to keep track of the time," Lynn told me. Confused and a little dazed, I pulled my watch off my wrist and passed it into the car. "Thanks," she said, and the car sped off.

I thought, "I may have just been robbed." But in a nice way.

Our small church-sponsored college held an annual Sadie Hawkins event in the fall. (Note that it wasn't a Sadie Hawkins *Dance*—dancing wasn't allowed.)

I had no idea who or what Sadie Hawkins was. I was told that, for this event, the girls would invite the guys instead of the other way around. Polite guys followed the "rule" that they must go to the Sadie Hawkins event with the first girl who asked him.

Construction on a dormitory had just been completed at the new campus. Males were all on the second floor, and females on the first. The dorm parents' apartment and a lounge with a piano, TV, chairs, couches, and tables were also on the first floor.

One Monday morning in the fall, word had spread on the guy's floor that the women were waiting in the lounge downstairs to surprise us with an invitation to be their date to the Sadie Hawkins event. We devised a strategy to go quickly through the crowd, covering our ears so we couldn't hear invitations from other girls until our first choice for a date had a chance to invite us. Very mature, right?

I walked into the lounge, and there was that red-haired beauty, Mary McSwain, right in front of me, handing me an invitation card. It had a cute construction paper cutout of an ear of corn with the text, "You can take Steven out of the country, but you can't take the country out of Steven."

That did it—she understood me. I said yes, I would accept her invitation. It was at that point that I realized we were beginning a relationship. So much for not getting tied down!

Mary and I found inexpensive ways to spend time together—walking downtown and window shopping. We often took walks through Johnson Park in Norfolk since we, like most students, couldn't afford to go to movies or eat out. We spent hours discussing our families, schools, hometowns, hopes, and dreams.

One evening, the moon was full as we walked along the river that ran through the park. I stopped to look up at the sky and began describing what the moon had looked like through my little telescope—how beautiful it was, how bright and smooth it looked, and yet, up close, it was rough, rugged, and mountainous.

Mary's face was just 12 inches from mine. She was watching me tell my story—focused and interested. She appeared to be impressed with my knowledge of astronomy. She understood exactly how I felt.

I leaned in for our first kiss. Her lips were so soft, and she was so beautiful. We dated exclusively throughout the school year.

Though there were some bumps when summer came, exactly one year later, on another stroll through Johnson Park, I took a deep breath and asked Mary to marry me.

She said yes!

P.S. In case you were wondering, I did get my watch back!

Mary and I on one of our first dates —the college's fall formal

9
Walk Hand in Hand with Me

For once in my life, my mom totally approved of my choice of a boyfriend. I used to tease her, accusing her of liking Steve better than me. We were engaged exactly one year after our first date. (So much for not getting tied down.)

As much as my mom liked Steve, she thought we were too young to get married. We were both 19, just a few months away from our 20th birthdays. We thought we were very mature and totally ready for marriage. Mom finally came around, or at least she figured out we wouldn't change our minds, so she went along with our plan.

Steve's dad Silas had to sign for him to get a marriage license because, at that time, men had to be 21 to marry in Wisconsin. I didn't need a parent's signature because women only had to be 18. Interesting. Maybe the powers-that-be thought that young women were more mature. Or perhaps women were thought to have less responsibility in a relationship than men, who were generally the wage earners.

We were married at my home church on the evening of May 29, 1971. In my father's absence, my brother Mike rang the church bell seven times at 7 p.m. and offered me his arm to walk me down the aisle. As we started the relatively short trip, guests stood and turned to watch.

In my father's absence, my brother, Michael, walked me down the aisle.

I suddenly realized that all eyes were on me, and I was terrified, as evidenced by the wedding photo snapped at that moment. I somehow made it down the aisle without fainting. Steve sang "Walk Hand in Hand with Me" to start the ceremony as we faced each other and held hands. The pastor of my childhood church (and my former heartthrob's father) officiated at our ceremony.

We exchanged silver bands engraved inside with the title of a song by the Carpenters, "We've Only Just Begun." The idea of engraving our rings came from one of my favorite books, a story about Mary Todd and Abraham Lincoln, whose wedding rings were engraved with the words "Love is Eternal." The Lincolns' inscription was, perhaps, a little weightier than words from a pop song, but at the age of not-quite 20, it was meaningful to us. The song was sung by a friend during the ceremony.

We honeymooned in northern Minnesota at a little cabin on Leech Lake near the town of Walker. We planned the trip while imagining looking over the lake from our balcony, relaxing on the beach, and maybe taking a boat out.

At least two things are wrong with that daydream and the destination. First, who takes a trip to northern Minnesota at the end of May? It was cold, cloudy, and blustery the whole time we were there. Second, we don't fish, which is why most people go to Leech Lake.

We were awakened every morning at 6 a.m. by the sound of fishing boats starting their engines. After turning out the lights at night, we heard a similar, very loud, and constant buzzing. We jumped out of bed, turned on the lights, and saw dozens of large mosquitos on the walls and ceiling of the cabin. It was certainly a honeymoon to remember.

We returned to college soon after our Leech Lake trip, living in married students' housing. Steve was studying to be a minister and was serving as an interim pastor for a little church in Akron, Iowa.

I had always enjoyed reading and creative writing throughout my grade school and high school years, so I decided to pursue a journalism degree. I sailed through the first two years of college, taking only classes I liked—writing, English, and literature. No math or science.

I was still a long way from a degree after my sophomore year. Two years later, when I should have been a senior about to graduate, I decided that we should have a baby instead of finishing college.

It seemed like such a great idea. I loved babies! I loved shopping for little pink and blue things! We didn't have the option of finding out the baby's gender in 1971, so I bought both. It would be so much fun to be the first of the couples in married student housing to have a baby. I had done a lot of babysitting in high school, so I considered myself experienced. I'd read somewhere that babies slept most of the time, so how hard could it be? And if we needed some "us" time, we'd just hire a sitter.

What could go wrong with our carefully thought-out plan?

10
Baby's Got Blue Eyes

Our first child, Joseph Steven Steele, was born on a Sunday evening in July 1973 in Norfolk, Nebraska. I had chosen his name when I was in high school, six years before he was born. I thought it was a name he could grow into: Joey as a toddler, Joe as a high school football player, and Joseph as an adult, maybe a doctor or lawyer.

We went to the hospital on July 14, certain our baby would be born within the hour. Twenty-four hours later, Joey finally arrived. He had red hair, as expected, and startling blue eyes. I was sure he would have brown eyes—mine are brown, and Steve's are green. But my mom and Steve's dad had those same clear blue eyes.

There were many special moments during our week-long hospital stay, the average length of time new mothers were hospitalized in the early '70s. Today, it's almost a same-day procedure.

A memory that will stay with me forever occurred on our fifth evening at the hospital. Back then, newborns were brought to their moms only at feeding times, and then they were rolled back to the nursery in their little plastic bassinets.

Steve came every night after his classes and his shift at work to visit me and see baby Joey. On Wednesday, though, there was a church softball game, so I encouraged him to go and help the team instead of coming to the hospital.

When softball night rolled around, I was feeling lonely and a little homesick, due mostly to knowing that Steve wouldn't be coming to visit. Maybe a touch of the "baby blues." I walked down to the end of the hallway so my roommate wouldn't see my tears, and I stood at the window looking out. There was absolutely no reason to feel sad, I told myself. I was delighted with this adorable red-haired, blue-eyed bundle. Pull yourself together, I told myself.

As I wiped away my tears, I saw a red Ford Pinto pull into the hospital parking lot, and Steve stepped out. He had decided that he'd rather spend the evening with his wife and baby than play softball. I had never loved and appreciated him more than at that moment.

When we took our new baby home three days later, my mom and her mom, Grandma Rosson, were waiting to greet us at our apartment and to meet Joey, Mom's first grandchild. Although I was a little sad to see them go when they left for home in Wisconsin a few days later, I was looking forward to it being just the three of us.

On the day Steve returned to school and his job, I was alone for the first time with Joey. There were no nurses to wheel him away to the nursery, no parents to offer advice, no roommate to help the time pass, and no husband to encourage or provide support.

Much to my dismay, our beautiful baby cried all day long. There was nothing I could do to soothe him. I thought there must be something seriously wrong with him. Maybe Joey wasn't getting enough milk. Maybe he was sick or in pain. I wondered if I should call 911.

When Steve came home, he took the baby in his arms and sang softly to his son. Joey was asleep in just a few minutes. I didn't know whether to be relieved or upset that I, his mother, couldn't comfort him. Steve seemed to have the magic touch. Joey began to sleep a little more as he got older, although never as many hours as the baby books said newborns usually slept.

After Steve graduated with a Bachelor of Sacred Literature degree, we decided to move from the Midwest to Upper East Tennessee so that he could standardize his degree to become a teacher. His brother, Tim, attended the same college, and a sister, Virginia, and her family lived nearby. They offered to let us stay at their home until we found a place of our own to rent.

Steve and I packed our four-week-old baby and everything we owned in our bright red Ford Pinto and his parents' pickup to begin the long trip from Nebraska to Tennessee. We should have been stressed or at least nervous about taking such a big step in our lives, but I only remember being excited to start this new adventure.

Steve got a job selling shoes at a local department store when he wasn't in class. I looked for a much-needed money-making opportunity that would allow me to work from home and was hired by a telemarketing firm to do surveys and polls over the phone. It was an interesting experience.

There's one phone conversation I remember specifically. The survey was about smoking. In Tennessee in the '70s, nearly everyone smoked or chewed tobacco. In this phone call, I interviewed a pleasant-sounding woman in her forties. One of the questions I was required to ask was: "How did you start smoking?"

I heard her giggle self-consciously before honestly answering, "Well, I started chewing (tobacco) first, and then I graduated to smoking!" She'd like to quit, she told me, but she didn't think it was something she'd be able to do.

A highlight of our time in Tennessee was the day I got my driver's license. I was 22 years old. When people asked why I waited so long, my usual story is that when I was in high school, my older sister and younger brother had their licenses, so I did not need to drive. But the truth is that the thought of being behind the wheel terrified me. I'd had driver's ed and passed with flying colors, yet I felt totally incompetent to drive by myself.

However, living in Tennessee with a new baby and a husband who was gone for long days meant I might have to shop for groceries, take the baby to the doctor by myself, or run other errands. So, Steve took me driving a few times to practice.

It was challenging because our Pinto had a 4-speed manual transmission. My biggest concern was stopping on a hill (and there were lots of them in Tennessee) for a red light. When the light turned green, I had to let up on the clutch and accelerate just enough to move the car slowly into the intersection. If I released the clutch too quickly, the car would suddenly jerk forward and sometimes kill the engine. So embarrassing! With lots of practice, my performance improved. Some. It was time to get my license.

On the appointed day, we drove to the courthouse, the only flat piece of land on the edge of town where there was very little traffic. I took the written test and passed. Then came the part I feared the most—the driving test.

The person conducting the test got into my car and instructed me to go straight to the end of the block and then take a right, which I did. So far, so good. Then he told me to go to the end of that block and turn right. He gave me the same instructions two more times, and we were back in front of the courthouse. I had passed! My "driving test" was to drive around the block!

Living in Tennessee was a special time for us. We were able to spend quality time with Steve's brother and also with his sister's family. I babysat for their two little boys and grew to be very fond of them. We enjoyed touring through the Appalachian Mountains and the beautiful countryside.

Steve graduated with a BA in Education after three semesters. During those 15 months, we lived in low-income housing, qualified for food stamps, and barely made ends meet.

We had lived below the poverty line throughout our marriage but thought we were rich. We were young and healthy, we had a beautiful baby, and we had each other. What else could we possibly need?

Our first family photo with baby Joey was taken by traveling photographers at a local department store.

11
How Can I Be Sure?

The year was 1970. I was returning to college after spending the summer working at a job in Iowa while Mary was home in Wisconsin. Simon and Garfunkel's hit "Bridge Over Troubled Water" was playing on the radio.

The first day of classes was a few days off, but I came back to Norfolk early, looking forward to finalizing my class schedule, searching for a part-time job, and checking in with the wrestling and track coach at the junior college.

It had been an important three months for me. I had never lived alone and been in complete control of my life before. Never had I been without family or friends living near me. There had always been someone close I could turn to for advice, though I didn't often ask for any. Their simple presence, perhaps, was reassurance enough. I set my own schedule and prioritized my responsibilities.

How Can I Be Sure?

I had never traveled alone before, but I mapped out a route to Readstown, Wisconsin, to visit Mary twice that summer. I stopped whenever I saw things that interested me. It was the first time I had been close to independence.

As I returned to college for my sophomore year and parked at the dormitory, I was thinking about Mary. I wondered how she felt about "us."

When I visited her during the summer in Readstown, I thought things were okay between us. I met Mary's mom, Betty, who seemed to like me. I loved the town and fell in love with southwest Wisconsin. Things were good—at least when I was with Mary. But after my first trip there, I sensed some hesitation on her part about our relationship.

Once again, "How can I be sure in a world that's constantly changing?" played in my mind. I wasn't sure about my career choice, the military involvement in Vietnam, and now my relationship with Mary. It seemed everything around me was on an unsure footing.

Before heading back to college that summer, I had been working at a TV station. I cleaned the studios, swept the floors, mopped, dusted, and helped with studio setup. Someone had to erase the weather map with all the writing, symbols, and temperatures! (No computer graphics in those days.)

The draft caused unrest throughout the country—many Americans opposed the war. Those who supported it clashed with war protesters, and some demonstrations became violent. The Kent State protest took place in May 1970. National Guard troops fired at unarmed protestors, killing four citizens. It was a confusing and sad time for our country.

July 1, 1970, was a tense day for me. My birthdate was one of those included in this second lottery. I had to examine what I believed about the war, the safety of our country, and our responsibility to protect freedom worldwide. Was it our responsibility? Could the type of freedom guaranteed under our Constitution survive abroad?

I was listening closely to the draft lottery drawings as I cleaned. There were two hand-cranked baskets: one with draft priority numbers 1 through 366, the other with dates of the year including February 29. My gut was in knots. I had decided I would serve if drafted. I believed it was important to trust our country's leadership and foreign policy since there was an alarming spread of dictatorship worldwide.

I heard the announcer call my birthdate as I worked. I paused and watched, mesmerized. Then the capsule with my draft position number was drawn: 270. It was high enough that I didn't need to worry about being drafted, and I breathed a sigh of relief. That anxiety was removed. I felt bad for the guys selected, knowing many didn't want to go, but the majority went and served anyway. I'm not sure there is anyone who would really want to fight in a war with the objective of killing people.

Sadly, those who served in that controversial and divisive conflict (it was never officially called a "war") didn't receive a hero's welcome when they returned home. Although they had fought for their country to defend our freedom and many were injured in battle, the returning soldiers were sometimes looked on almost as traitors.

The scenes on the evening news of soldiers getting off airplanes greeted by protesters tore at my conscience. They didn't start the war, and they didn't want the war. They deserved so much more.

Mary arrived on campus a few days after I did, and we finally had a chance to be together, to walk, talk, and process. I think she saw that summer as an important time to confirm where her life was heading and who she wanted in her future. But her hesitation about our relationship seemed to have been resolved, and it was clear to me that in her mind and heart, I was the one with whom she wanted to spend the rest of her life. Four weeks later, I asked her to marry me, and nine months after that, we were married.

In the fall of '71, Mary and I returned to Norfolk as a married couple to finish our last two years of college. Included in the ministerial education I was pursuing, the college encouraged older students to work with small churches in the area around Norfolk. I found a weekend home with a small congregation in Akron, Iowa.

A rookie student minister hits the books while preparing for the Sunday sermon.

I benefitted from the wise leadership of many in that congregation of believers. I came to understand much more about the ministry from that experience. I am certain that the congregation taught me more than they learned from me. For that, I am forever grateful. Together we kept the church house doors open and offered a place for believers to gather, have formal worship, and share communion.

In that mix of faith and service, however, I wondered if the located "professional" ministry was right for me. I did a lot of soul-searching during that time, which was mostly the purpose of the student pastor experience.

During the four years Mary and I spent in Norfolk, we received a wide and varied education. Besides "book learning," we also learned through our life experiences. We developed our faith and trust in God, as well as our faith and trust in each other. Considering all the changes occurring in our lives, the bond of love through our faith was a powerful force pointing us in the right direction.

We stayed in our little apartment on campus through the summer after graduating in May 1973 with a Bachelor of Sacred Literature Degree. I decided to continue my studies and pursue a Health, Physical Education, and Recreation degree. Our new baby would be born in July, and we planned to move to Milligan College in northeast Tennessee in August.

I didn't know which direction God would take us, but I felt very good about education as a career. I liked school, although I was not the best student. I learned so much from my teachers, who seemed to want the best for us students. And I appreciated how they had influenced my life in a positive direction.

Shortly after graduation, a young pastor asked me what I would do with my new ministerial degree. I told him of our plans to go to Milligan College, Tennessee, to pursue an education degree, and become a teacher. He responded, "Don't you think the Lord's work is more important?"

His comment was like a punch to the stomach. "God needs good teachers and coaches in schools, too," I managed to reply. I grew up believing we all are doing God's work every day. I often reminded myself of my answer to the young pastor in the years that followed.

During my first year of teaching middle school students, I would find out just how true those words were.

12
Double Your Pleasure, Double Your Fun

We left Tennessee and headed back to the Midwest in January 1975. Steve had earned his BA in Health, Physical Education, and Recreation in addition to the Bachelor of Sacred Literature degree he completed in Nebraska. We hoped he'd find a teaching position, but openings were scarce in the middle of the school year.

Steve's parents, Silas and Doris, graciously invited us to stay with them on the family farm until we had our own home. It was a generous offer considering we had an 18-month-old and a new baby on the way. Doris was a gentle soul, kind and welcoming. I didn't have any qualms about us living with my mother-in-law. I used to joke that if I ever decided to run home to mother, it would be his mother and not mine.

My well-meaning but overbearing mom loved her children,

but as I have mentioned, she wasn't always the easiest person to live with. Or maybe I just remember the tense moments more vividly. Either way, Mom's personality changed over the years when her load of single-mom responsibilities became lighter, and after 20 years of raising children by herself, she, too, could experience more freedom in her life.

It was a rough winter in Northwest Iowa from a weather standpoint. The blizzard of 1975 left 12 to 16 inches of snow blown by 60 mph winds creating snowdrifts as high as 10 ft. around the Steele farm.

Our second baby was due in the middle of March, and I was worried I might go into labor during the blizzard. What if we couldn't make the 20-mile trip to the hospital on the snow-and-ice-covered roads? Steve tried to calm my fears by saying confidently, "I'll drive you to the hospital in the tractor—it has a cab and a heater."

Obviously, he had never experienced labor. He hadn't considered how a pregnant woman in labor might be extremely uncomfortable bouncing around on a tractor seat. One big bump could result in a very quick delivery. As exciting as it might sound, I didn't want to be in the Guinness Book of Records for being the first woman to have a baby in a J.I. Case 1070 cab.

Fortunately, it didn't come to that. By the time March 14th rolled around, the roads had been cleared, and the weather had improved considerably. I woke up that morning with vague aches and pains, but I didn't say anything to Steve about the possibility that I might be in labor before he left for work. Doris and I planned to go shopping in nearby Cherokee that day, so I didn't mention it to her either because I didn't want our shopping trip to be canceled. After weeks of being snowed in at the farm, I was ready for a change of scenery.

At about 4 p.m., however, I was beginning to regret my decision to go shopping. I waited in the car while Doris bought groceries—thankfully, our last stop before heading back to the farm. We arrived just a few minutes before Steve got home from work. I told him that I was having serious contractions and that we needed to get to the hospital ASAP. I gave him about three minutes to change out of his work clothes before heading back to Cherokee, leaving little Joey at the farm with Grandma and Grandpa.

We were almost to the hospital when I remembered that Steve hadn't had any supper, so I told him to pull into a restaurant's drive-through and ask for "the quickest thing on the menu." He choked down his burger while driving the last mile to the hospital.

I was actually looking forward to spending time in the hospital's new labor rooms because they were equipped with televisions, which was rare in the '70s. I was especially excited because my favorite Friday night show, "The Rockford Files" with James Garner, would be on.

Imagine my disappointment when I realized that the show had been pre-empted by the girls' state basketball finals. Coming from Wisconsin, where there were no organized sports for girls, at least not in smaller schools, I thought Iowa girls' basketball was kind of a joke. (My apologies to all the female basketball players everywhere, including my daughter, who was quite the hoopster in high school!)

Instead of watching basketball, Steve polished my toenails. I told him that if I was going to be looking at my feet for hours, I at least wanted to have pretty toes to look at. I would have polished them myself, but as you can probably picture, there was no way I'd be able to reach my toes.

As it turned out, we didn't spend much time in the labor

room. Aaron Michael Steele was born less than two hours after we arrived at the hospital. He was a beautiful baby—dark brown eyes, long lashes, smooth skin, and, of course, red hair.

Steve called home, and when his mom answered the phone, he asked to speak to Joey. His parents later told us that as soon as Joey heard the news, his eyes got big; he dropped the receiver and announced proudly, "I have a new baby brother!"

We had only a few euphoric hours before the doctors told us that Aaron had some blood issues. My blood type is O- and Steve's is A+ which we soon learned is not always compatible. The doctor explained that if the baby has type A blood and the mother has O, the mom's blood cells can develop antibodies that may attack the baby's blood cells and cause jaundice. We knew about the incompatibility of Rh-negative versus Rh-positive blood types, but we hadn't considered the possibility of A/O blood disease being a threat to our second baby.

Aaron's bilirubin count was dangerously high the day after his birth, and we were told he would need a blood transfusion. He was taken by ambulance to Sioux City, which had a bigger hospital with a neonatal intensive care unit.

I told Steve that I was leaving the hospital and following the ambulance to Sioux City, and I didn't care what the doctors said. Back then, the usual hospital stay after a normal delivery for mom and baby was 5-7 days, and I had been at the hospital just 12 hours. Fortunately, the doctors agreed to discharge me. They probably thought that was less risky than telling a determined new mom with raging hormones that she couldn't go with her baby.

The doctors ordered another blood test when we got to the

Sioux City hospital. Results showed that the bilirubin count had decreased, so they decided to hold off on the transfusion. Instead, they put Aaron, an 8 lb. 6 oz. otherwise healthy-looking baby (except for his yellow skin tone) in the NICU, where he would be closely monitored.

Seeing Aaron among the tiny preemies with tubes hooked up to them made us realize how blessed we were that our baby's issues could be treated without invasive procedures. He only needed to be kept under ultraviolet lamps that would, hopefully, bring his bilirubin count down without a transfusion.

Aaron's condition continued to improve. We were allowed to hold him, and I could nurse him. Three days later, we had a phone call from the hospital before we left the farm for our daily trip to Sioux City. It was a nurse saying we could take our sweet baby home. I was so surprised and relieved that I burst into tears of joy.

A few weeks after Aaron's birth, we moved from the farm to the community where Steve had taken a position as pastor of a small church, as there were no openings for teachers in the middle of the second semester. His starting pay was $50 a week. There were some perks: we would live in the parsonage at no cost, and the church would pay our utilities. A generous member of the church, a local farmer, kept our freezer full of meat. Later, Steve's salary would be raised to $75. Somehow, we got by.

Again, I found myself home alone, but this time with both a new baby and a 21-month-old. Fortunately, Aaron was not as high-maintenance as his older brother, especially when it came to sleeping. Perhaps that's typical of a second child—parents don't have as much time to shower attention on child No. 2 as they may have done with their firstborn.

When it was naptime, we put Aaron in his crib with a music tape of Bach concertos that he seemed to like. He would talk to himself until he fell asleep. I would say silently to him, "Thank you, thank you, Aaron."

Then I would pick up his older brother and rock him for what seemed like forever until he finally gave up and closed his eyes. I think we rocked Joey to sleep for naps and every night at bedtime until he was two years old.

Twenty-seven months later, our young sons would welcome a new sibling. But that's for another chapter.

We put a lot of miles on this rocker when Joe and Aaron were little.

13
Brown-Eyed Girl

The mid-'70s were a time of big changes for our little family. Besides Steve getting his teaching degree but finding no teacher openings, moving back to Steve's parents' farm in Iowa until our baby was born, and accepting a call to pastor a small church in a nearby community, we were also learning just how challenging it is to have a newborn and a toddler.

Joey was 22 months old, and Aaron was just three weeks old when we loaded up the Pinto and moved for the third time in 18 months. The two boys got along well as toddlers; watching them play and grow together was a joy for us.

Both boys had red hair and were close in size. People often asked if they were twins. Though they looked alike, we began to notice their personalities weren't identical as they got older. Joey was (usually) good-natured and easygoing. Aaron was more pensive and serious, maybe even intuitive. We often wondered what he was thinking and feeling. With Joe, you knew—his face reflected his feelings.

For his first Christmas, we gave Aaron a Fischer Price boy doll. We thought it might bring out his softer side. The doll had red hair and was dressed in blue jeans, a striped shirt, high-top tennis shoes, and a letter jacket. Coincidentally, Fischer Price had named the doll "Joey."

When Aaron tore the wrap off the package and saw the red-haired doll, he said with a smile, "Doh-Doh!" It was what he called his brother because, at 18 months, he couldn't pronounce "Joey." He seemed very pleased with his new friend and often carried the Joey doll around with him.

As Aaron got older and it was no longer cool to carry a doll around, he tried to slip Joey onto a table at one of our garage sales. Although the doll had served its purpose, I couldn't bear to let it go. I grabbed it off the table, rescuing it from shoppers looking for a bargain, and I put it away for safekeeping. Twenty-two years later, I would give Aaron's soon-to-be-wife Nicole the Joey doll as an engagement gift.

Aaron and Nicole with the Joey doll in 2022

Steve continued to look for teaching jobs while serving as a pastor. With each passing day, he became more convinced that the ministry was not the right career for him. But when the school year started in the fall, he'd had no offers to interview for the few teaching positions available.

Two weeks into the 1976 year, Steve got a call from a friend of his family who was the principal at Crestland Schools in Early, Iowa. He asked Steve to interview for a position that had suddenly opened. A first-year teacher had decided to throw in the towel after just 15 days in the classroom due to the anxiety it was causing him. Interestingly, that would-be teacher got a job as a policeman in a bigger community—not usually considered a low-stress career.

Steve interviewed and was offered the position. He would teach science, math, and physical education with coaching. When he came home with a copy of the contract, he showed me that his yearly salary would be $6,500. I turned to him, eyes wide open in disbelief, and said, "Steve, what will we do with all that money?" It sounded like a fortune, but I don't remember having any difficulty spending it.

In the meantime, we discovered that our third child would be born in June 1977. We wanted to move to Early before our baby was born, so we rented a cute two-bedroom house in town. Steve agreed to continue serving as pastor on weekends—it was a short commute—until the church could find a replacement for him.

We thoroughly enjoyed living in the small village of Early. We got to know several other couples our age and had young families. We all took turns hosting casual social gatherings and shared babysitting. Steve was enjoying his new job, although teaching, coaching, and serving as pastor part-time meant the days were long, and he didn't spend much time at home with his growing family.

Brown-Eyed Girl

I was awakened by mild contractions on Sunday, July 26, 1977. When I told Steve I was in labor, he seemed a little disappointed. He had spent hours working on his sermon and was looking forward to preaching that morning.

He asked me, "Are you sure?" (Maybe because he'd heard me use that line twice before and then had to wait long hours at the hospital....) I replied that I was very sure.

We called Steve's parents, who drove to Early immediately to take Joey and Aaron back to the farm. Then we called the doctor. He told us that it would probably be a while with my previous history and that we should wait before going to the hospital.

We waited nervously until almost noon before starting the 20-mile trip to the hospital. By the time we'd gone halfway, I knew we'd waited too long. The last 10 miles were the longest 10 minutes of my life.

Steve was driving considerably faster than the speed limit, thinking that if he got picked up, we would get a police escort to the hospital. I told him we didn't have time to pull over and explain our situation to a cop. Besides, I didn't think flying over railroad tracks at 90 mph would help slow down labor.

When we got to the E.R., the nurses recognized that I could deliver any moment. They rushed me past the labor rooms and into the delivery room. When the doctor arrived 20 minutes later, two nurses put on his gown as he delivered our baby.

I'll never forget the conversation that followed:

Steve: "It's a girl!"

Me: "Are you sure?"

Steve, laughing: "Yes, I'm sure!" (Never mind that he'd had anatomy and physiology classes in college. And two little boys at home.)

Me: "Is it a girl? Really?"

Doctor: "Yes, it's a girl."

Considering the doctor had been to med school, I figured he should know.

When it finally sunk in, I was euphoric. For almost nine months, I was certain we were having a third boy. Moms-to-be back then didn't know the gender of their babies in advance unless an amniocentesis was needed.

I wasn't just trying to spare myself any potential disappointment. I'd had a gut feeling this baby was a boy. So much for my mother's intuition and my longtime belief that I was "a little bit psychic."

We named our baby girl Laura Ellyn Steele after two maternal great-grandmothers: "Laura" after Steve's Grandma Fredenburg and "Ellyn" after my Grandma Rosson.

We left the hospital with little Laura after three days. Steve's parents brought the boys home that afternoon to meet our new baby. Joey and Aaron had been playing outside at the farm and were covered with dirt. (Grandma Steele didn't want to "spoil their fun by making them take a bath.") The boys couldn't wait to hug and touch their new sister with grimy little hands. We put them in the bathtub and scrubbed them clean. Only then did they hold their baby sister.

Even as a newborn, Laura had a way of looking at us when we talked to her like she understood far more than she should have been able to. It was almost eerie how perceptive she seemed to be.

The next weekend we took our first trip as a family of five, going to a family reunion. I remember thinking how incredibly blessed we were as we drove through the countryside. We had the perfect family we'd always dreamed of: two boys and a girl. It sounds old-fashioned and a little sexist now, but I always thought it would be nice to have our boys first so they could look out for their little sister.

As it turned out, Laura wasn't the type of girl who needed anyone to look out for her. She learned very quickly to take care of herself. As a toddler, we could tell she would not be a namby-pamby girl.

Laura enjoyed her dolls but loved doing whatever the boys did—sometimes much to their dismay: collecting baseball cards, shooting hoops in the driveway, or playing touch football in the yard. Sports would continue to be important to her for decades to come.

Laura works on her catching skills with Joe and Aaron.

14
The Long and Winding Road

Mary has shared from her perspective about our time after living in Tennessee. Here's my take on that first year.

With all the uncertainty about my future, it was good to feel the security of the farm and to have a roof over our heads. My foster brother, Keith, was home for a few days before leaving for the U.S. Marine Corps. I think Dad appreciated the extra help around, which was good for what lay ahead.

Two weeks later, a blizzard of historical proportions hit northwest Iowa. Heavy snow, high winds, and very low temperatures created dangerous conditions. Any uncovered skin would start to freeze in a minute or two. Keith and I carried hay bales across the road for two long days to feed the cattle. We couldn't use farm equipment to haul bales because the snow was too deep. Dad made sure the water pipes were thawed and flowing.

It was a hard winter, with snow, wind, and cold from January to March. We were expecting our second baby in 10 weeks. I recall boasting to Mary that if she went into labor during a blizzard, we would just jump in the heated cab of our Case 1070 and go to the hospital in Cherokee, 18 miles away.

As a backup plan, I felt confident I could deliver our baby at home. I had just studied the physiology of childbirth in an anatomy class at Milligan College. I had listened closely and taken copious notes, so I felt qualified. Piece of cake!

Those two options were our only choices in a blizzard.

To earn a degree in education is one thing, but to find teaching jobs mid-year is another. In the evenings, I searched the newspapers and wrote applications to the few schools with openings. In the meantime, I found employment with a farm equipment manufacturer building snow blowers. Not surprisingly, snow removal equipment sold well that winter.

Aaron was born safely on March 14, 1975, at the Cherokee Hospital as planned, but his A/O blood type issues were unexpected. Mary shared how he was transported to a bigger hospital for a transfusion. Doctors there decided instead to try to "burn off" the bilirubin produced to acceptable levels under UV lights.

It worked! No transfusion was needed. We were ecstatic and relieved. Aaron's birth highlighted the fact that—as grateful as we were for my parents sharing their home with us for three months—I needed to find a way for our family to be on our own again. That was my goal when I left home for college, and I didn't want to depend on my parents, especially now that I was married with two children.

Just after Aaron's birth, it happened that an opening for a pastor at a small church in northwest Iowa became available. I knew I wanted to be a classroom teacher and coach, but I hadn't received any job offers despite all my efforts. When the ministerial position became available, I thought maybe God was trying to put me on a different path—God's path. Not mine.

I interviewed and preached a Sunday sermon, after which the congregation voted, and I was asked to be their minister. I wanted to follow where God was leading, so Mary and I together decided that I should accept the position.

Without dwelling on background details, I soon discovered this was a troubled congregation. Power struggles among members over non-spiritual issues often create division in church groups—issues like purchasing an organ or buying new carpeting and other cosmetic decisions.

After six months, I wondered why God had led me there. What did I, a 23-year-old pastor, have to offer those elders and deacons who were my dad's age or older?

They were good people individually but couldn't agree on much together. I thought that if we could get the key players together in the same room, face to face, we could start a dialogue and work through our problems. I invited board members to our house for a heart-to-heart discussion, certain that we could work this out through communication.

What followed was the longest silence I have ever experienced. My naivety was obvious—and humiliating. I thought God would work something good in us that night, but despite my prayerful appeal and prodding for discussion, no one—not one—talked. None shared their thoughts or showed a willingness to find a solution.

Ultimately, they all left in absolute silence. As in today's political arena, no one wanted to look weak. Privately, church people said to me, "This is nothing against you, but we just can't go back to that church." It was at that point I realized I was just spinning my wheels.

All I could say to them was, "You must do what you must do. I understand." Half the membership left the church, and I was left with the nagging question: What responsibility did I bear?

That was the situation on a Friday evening, the end of the first week in September 1976. I was playing with Joey and Aaron in our living room, laughing and tickling them while despairing about the church. I didn't think I could do anything to bring the congregation back together.

"God," I asked, "is this the way it will always be?"

At that exact moment, I was jolted by the sound of the phone ringing. The call was from a former teacher, coach, and family friend. Without any chit-chat, he got right to the point of his call. He said, "I don't know if you've heard, but I'm principal at Crestland High School in Early now. One of our teachers suddenly resigned. I know you're the minister there, but are you still interested in teaching?"

I was stunned by the timing of the call. In my heart, I knew it was God. He had something else in mind for me. "Yes," I said immediately. "I want to teach."

I drove to Early Saturday morning for an interview with the superintendent and signed a contract at the end of our meeting. I started my new job the following Monday morning as a teacher and coach at Crestland Junior/Senior High School. My schedule included 7th and 8th-grade math, science, and physical education, as well as supervising the lunchroom and a study hall.

I had never considered teaching junior high students. If you aspire to coach varsity athletics, then teaching the high school students that you will also be coaching is the best situation. Athletes learn personal expectations and values in their coach's classroom that will hopefully transfer onto the field.

Teaching 8th graders about plate tectonics

As it turned out, I enjoyed the younger kids, who were still pliable in attitude and thought. I worked with older athletes in P.E., so I had the best of both worlds.

I was the assistant football and head girls' track coach that first school year. Football and track were the two sports I had always wanted to coach. But, like teaching younger students, I had never thought about coaching girls' track, partly because we didn't have a girls' track team at my high school. Like my experience teaching younger kids, I discovered I enjoyed coaching the girls. They were enthusiastic, and they worked hard. Everything I'd hoped for had come together.

Life couldn't have been better for us as a family. I was still pastoring at the church, but my position was limited to weekends only. After each Sunday service, the board treasurer would hand me a $50 check and say, "You make more per hour than anyone I know." He meant it as a joke. (I think.)

By the summer of 1979, I was feeling comfortable in my role as a teacher and coach. But my story with the church was not yet finished. I was presented with a new challenge that began with a phone call from the sheriff.

15
Happy Together

We were enjoying life in Early, Iowa, where Steve was teaching and coaching at Crestland Junior/Senior High School while he was still pastoring a small congregation 30 miles away on weekends. Our children made new friends quickly, were healthy and growing, and we were all happy.

When our family first moved to Early in 1976, the community had several churches and more than a dozen businesses, including a gas station, grocery store, clothing and gift shop, bank, elevator/feed mill, Hardware Hank, and sundries store. Its biggest business was the Payless Cashways lumber yard. It was one of the first to become part of that chain and was credited with implementing the Do It Yourself (DIY) concept.

Early was known for being an "artsy" community. It had an unusually high percentage of residents involved in the arts, including musicians, writers, poets, watercolor and oil artists, graphic artists, quilters, weavers, wood carvers, and crafters.

Happy Together

The summer before Joey started kindergarten in 1978, an ad in our local weekly newspaper, *The Early News*, caught my attention. The paper had been sold, leaving the office without staff. When the newspaper changed hands, the new publisher advertised for a part-time office assistant. The ad said, "Degree preferred."

I had completed two years of college right after graduating from high school and then put my education on hold. Instead, I chose to get married and have a family. Throughout the mid-1970s to early '80s, all of my time and energy went into caring for our three children and keeping up the house.

Although I didn't have a degree, I had taken several journalism classes and felt fairly confident about my writing skills. I interviewed for *The Early News* position and was hired. My title would be "office assistant," but no one else was in the office for me to *assist*. My title was changed three months later to "editor," although my job description stayed basically the same. I would be in charge of everything from writing all the stories to handling subscriptions. Even so, it was nice to be recognized as an editor.

A friend agreed to babysit Aaron, 4, and Laura, 2, while I worked 20 hours weekly. Millie had two little boys, so my kids were delighted to have playmates three days a week. The newspaper office was kitty-corner across from the older two-story fixer-upper house we had recently purchased to accommodate our growing family. It was a perfect situation for my first job after being a stay-at-home mom for five years.

The Early News covered local happenings—not any state or national news. As you might expect, there wasn't a lot of hard news locally to report. I was okay with that. I was more of a "lifestyles" reporter and not so much into hard news. It was a good place for me to get my feet wet in print journalism.

Early celebrated its centennial in July 1983, and to commemorate the occasion, *The Early News* printed an 84-page centennial edition, "People, Places, and Things." I put my heart and soul into that edition, doing all the writing, photography, layout, and research myself.

The special edition sold out three times, and we did several more press runs to keep up with sales. Finally, my boss, the publisher (and the one who operated the presses), said, "That's it. We can't run any more copies!"

After the event, we put out another special issue with photos of the centennial celebration. It was 32 pages and also sold out quickly. I was proud that all my hard work had paid off in terms of turning a profit for my boss, whom I admired and respected.

Past residents were invited to come back to Early for the centennial celebration, including several who had become famous. Janet Dailey, a well-known and prolific writer of romance novels, was one of those people. Born Janet Haradon, she was raised on a farm near Early. One of her first novels, *The Homeplace*, was set in Early.

I hadn't ever read a romance novel—to be honest, I avoided the whole genre—but I was excited to interview her because I knew she had an interesting backstory.

After graduating from high school, Janet attended secretarial school in Omaha before landing a job as secretary to the CEO of a construction and land development company. Janet married her boss, Bill Dailey, who was ten years older.

Three years later, in 1974, they decided to sell their business, retire, and travel the country in their silver Airstream RV.

They flipped a coin to determine which direction to go first—east or west. They flipped and headed west to Texas.

Janet spent most of her travel time reading boxes full of romance novels, frequently commenting to Bill that she "could write better than these authors!"

Tired of hearing that line repeatedly, Bill finally said something to the effect of: "Then start writing!" Only not quite so politely.

And so, she did, setting a goal of writing a book set in every state. When they got to each location, Bill researched the area so Janet could write about it. She wrote every day beginning at 4 a.m. and didn't stop until she had written at least 15 pages.

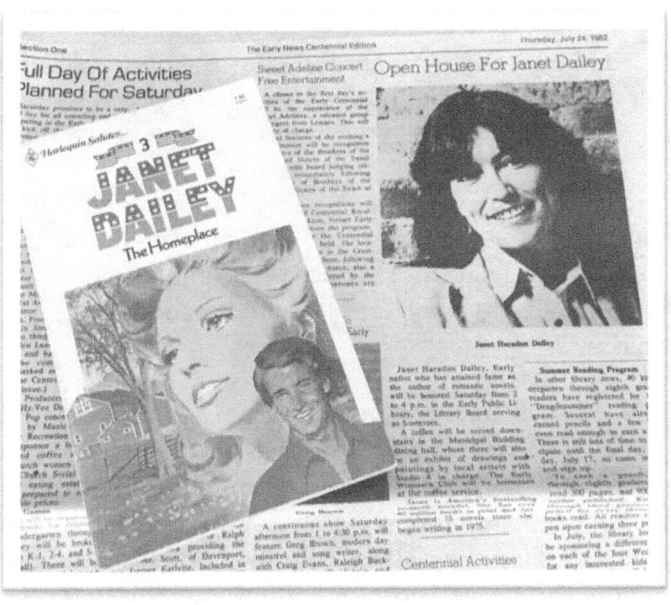

Janet Dailey's first book, "The Homeplace," was set in Early, Iowa, where she grew up.

Amazingly, she made no edits or revisions—her first draft was her final draft. (Compare that to this author—and maybe most authors—whose motto is: Revise, rewrite, and rip up the first dozen or so drafts.)

In 1975, Janet sold more than 80 million paperbacks. Over the years, she became one of the best-selling female authors in the country, writing more than 100 novels with 300 million copies sold in 19 languages in 98 countries. Janet was known for her strong, decisive characters, both male and female, and for her courage to confront controversial and important issues.

I remember only one hard news story I covered for *The Early News*. It was Saturday evening, November 13th, 1982. Steve and I had just gotten home from a social gathering, and I was getting ready for bed when I heard a loud BOOM that shook our house. I thought someone must be setting off fireworks (in November?). Steve's first thought was that the elevator had blown up. But I'll let him tell you that story in his next chapter since he spent as many hours covering it as I did.

Although a small newspaper in a small community, working at The Early News was enjoyable and satisfying. I learned photography and darkroom procedures, improved my writing skills, and realized I wanted to learn more about print journalism.

In 1984, 15 years after my first college experience, I enrolled part-time at Buena Vista University in Storm Lake, 20 miles north of Early. BVU had a mass communications program with excellent instructors. My classes were challenging and rewarding. Taking the classes confirmed that my main focus in continuing my education for a future career would be to become a better writer.

I decided to write as a correspondent for the *Sioux City*

Journal. I was given assignments, and I often came up with my own ideas for stories and pitched them to the editor. At the same time, I continued to work at *The Early News.*

A year later, I had the opportunity to work full-time at the *Journal.* That was a big step up for me, but as it turned out, I couldn't accept the position for reasons we will share in an upcoming chapter.

Like most small Midwestern towns, Early felt the effect of the downward turn in the economy during the '80s. In the first half of the decade, local businesses were forced to close their doors, including the only grocery store in town. Then the feds shut down the Early Savings Bank. There were several other closings and bankruptcies, and all were painful losses for the residents of the close-knit community where everyone knew everyone.

Seeing our town shrinking, many of our friends found new jobs and moved to bigger towns. I started to feel like we had been left behind and I encouraged Steve to apply for other teaching positions.

Steve was perfectly happy to stay in Early—he loved the community and his students. But with smaller class sizes every year, he knew that at some point, Crestland would have to consolidate with nearby schools. With any merger would come the reduction of staff. And so, he reluctantly applied to a few schools in bigger towns.

16
There's Got to Be a Morning After

The invention of the telephone, like that of television, brought incredible change to our culture and to the world. The telephone, though, has the innate ability to disrupt and intrude.

On the farm, I liked doing fieldwork on the tractor, hunting with the dog, and other activities where I could be alone with my thoughts. At home, the jarring intrusion of the telephone ring usually meant more work or bad news.

My friends and I never called each other. They might have called other friends in town who had time to go out for a bike ride, but that was never my situation. My family's mindset was that the phone was for important use only. However, I did find it interesting to sometimes listen in on our neighbors' party-line conversations.

There's Got to Be a Morning After

Many changes in my life began with the ring of the phone. Another such call was on a pleasant summer day in 1979. When the phone rang, I picked up the receiver, and the caller identified himself as a sheriff's officer. I immediately thought the worst—a car accident or a heart attack involving someone close to me. Instead, the news was of a different nature.

A married man and a married woman from the congregation I was still pastoring on weekends had been having an affair. One of the couples had separated, and it was not an amicable separation. Both were committed parents and couldn't agree on issues such as child custody and visitation arrangements.

Earlier that day, the mom had left the children at the father's home for a visit. When she came to pick them up, their father wouldn't let the kids leave. She told the sheriff that her ex-husband had a gun.

"Would you be okay with coming over to talk with the husband?" the officer asked me. "His ex-wife thinks he would listen to you because you are his pastor."

I was stunned, but I said I would drive over. I thought about the situation on the drive to their house. Domestic disputes can be dangerous, but I didn't think the personalities involved would be violent. However, I also knew that people do unexpected things when stressed. I asked myself, "What should I watch for? Will he be angry? Would he hurt the children or himself? What should I tell him that God could use to disarm this situation?"

About a quarter mile before I got to their home, I saw sheriff's cars parked along the road with officers standing there. I stopped and identified myself. The officer asked me again, "Are you sure about this situation? Are you comfortable with going in?"

"Yes, I am. It will be ok," I replied. I truly felt that way, yet nervous at the same time—weird. The officers had set up in a position where the husband couldn't see them and be aware that law enforcement was present. He also didn't know I was coming to talk to him.

The deputy handed me a radio which punctuated the gravity of the situation. "You have 15 minutes. If we don't hear from you in that time period, we **will** be coming in." He emphasized the word "will." His statement didn't help me to relax.

I drove to the house with my heart racing, not knowing what to expect, yet I couldn't believe this man would do anything violent. When I knocked, he opened the door and shook my hand like he was glad to see me and invited me inside.

I immediately showed him the radio the deputy had given me. Then I laid out the situation for him, watching his reaction. He seemed very surprised at my concern. As we visited, he said he hoped I would never think that he could do anything violent or harmful to the kids, himself, or anyone else.

I contacted the officer, who then came to the house and checked on the welfare of the children. He confirmed that the ex-wife would be coming for the children, and I was able to leave. That was the end of what might have been a tragedy but instead came to a peaceful conclusion. I was filled with relief.

It wasn't the telephone that disrupted the peacefulness of our quiet town of Early. On November 13, 1982, at 10:27 p.m., we heard an explosion that rattled the house. Some explosions are sharp and loud. This one was low and deep, which doesn't hurt your ears so much as it pounds your chest from the pressure waves it caused.

There's Got to Be a Morning After

I expected to see the grain elevator in flames as there had been several explosions caused by grain dust at feed mills in the area while harvest was winding down. I ran to the big picture window of our house on Walnut Street, expecting to see flames to the southwest. There were no flames in that direction, but the sky was bright to our northwest. Except for homes, the only structures to the northwest were the Methodist Church and the school.

We tucked the kids in bed, Mary grabbed the Early News camera, and we drove towards the bright sky to see what had happened.

The three-story brick school building looked as if a bomb had exploded in the middle of the structure. Essentially, that is exactly what had happened; only the "bomb" was natural gas.

Firefighters and emergency crews arrived at the scene from other towns to assist the Early Fire Department. Their priority was to find a way to shut down a broken gas line that was feeding the fire.

The firefighters were shooting water in and around that area to keep the rest of the building from burning. It was miserably cold, and the wind was blowing fiercely, adding to the difficulty of fighting the fire. Water was freezing in shiny sheets, and icicles formed where water dripped to the ground. The three-story chimney was the only structure left standing in the middle of the building.

I talked to students at the scene, who were shocked that anything like this could happen. We marveled at how lucky we were that no one was in or near the school at the time of the explosion. A teacher and her daughter had stopped in to pick up files just hours before.

This is all that was left of the Crestland Junior/Senior High School the day after the explosion.

Some of my students had tears in their eyes, knowing they would not graduate in this building that had always been there—a monument to their education and daily home away from home. It had always seemed so certain, secure, and permanent. Now what? As I talked to them, I searched for something I could share that might help them as they struggled with their feelings. I was surprised at the depth of their disappointment and sense of loss. I was just so glad this hadn't happened the previous day when school was in session.

The school board had already been discussing possible sharing programs and athletics with Schaller a few miles away. If the board decided to build a new school building, Early would have all new facilities to go with a recently built athletic complex. Hopefully, that would put them in a good position for a consolidated high school located in Early. It would be a positive step for the town.

However, there was the possibility that the board would decide not to rebuild and instead combine with another district, a disaster for us and Early.

After the explosion, the school board and community pulled together to develop a strategy so the students would continue their education with as little disruption as possible. The Methodist, Lutheran, and Presbyterian churches all offered their facilities. Within a few days, students returned to school, meeting in make-shift classrooms.

Even though our school was in a church building, I was still very satisfied teaching at Crestland. The class sizes were small enough that I could load all the 7th and 8th-grade science students onto a bus for field trips.

Even so, the handwriting was on the wall for teachers. Class sizes were as low as 14 in the 7th grade. If Crestland consolidated with another school, we might not have jobs in a few years.

It was clear that big changes were on the horizon for our

district, which forced me to think about how they would affect my job and family. Mary had begun to suggest that we consider moving to a larger town. She was anxious for us to find a more secure situation.

Like the pastoral position in '75, I sought God's guidance. I told Mary, "I will apply to any school with an opening that would fit me. If I get an interview, I will go and do my best. If God wants us to go, we will receive a job offer, and we will accept it."

In the early spring of 1985, I saw a notice for a position at Spencer Middle School for math, life science, and earth science, with assistant coaching positions in football and as track coordinator for the middle school. A perfect fit!

With a deep sigh, I dropped my application in the mailbox...

17
You Know It Don't Come Easy

Steve shared some of his memories from our time in Early, Iowa and our discussions about moving to a larger town with a bigger school. Although he was reluctant to leave the school and the community we had enjoyed for nine years, we were both concerned that teaching positions might be eliminated if there was a potential sharing agreement with another district.

I encouraged Steve to send out some applications and see what happened. The episode ends with Steve dropping an application in the mailbox.

Spoiler alert: Steve was hired to teach at Spencer Middle School.

We moved to Spencer in August 1985 when our kids were 8, 10, and 12. They were sad to leave their Early friends but excited to meet new ones.

Even before we moved, I had applied to the *Spencer Daily Reporter* for any newsroom position that might be open, part-time or full-time. I didn't have a degree, but I had worked for *The Early News* for six years, where I'd accumulated several Iowa Newspaper Association awards. In addition, I was taking classes part-time and working toward a degree in mass communications at Buena Vista University. I hoped my resume would be good enough, even without a degree, to convince my interviewers to hire me.

Although the *Reporter* had no openings in the newsroom, they hired me anyway. I was basically a typist: I typed courthouse news, weddings, obituaries, the community calendar, school activities, and anything else handed to me. Even though I wasn't reporting or writing, I was elated to work for a daily newspaper with seven people in the newsroom, plus staff in the front office, advertising, composition, press room, and printing. My elation with my new job was dampened somewhat when I sat in front of a computer for the first time. More about that later.

The agriculture reporter left within a few weeks after I started, and I was given his position. I had never lived on a farm (except for a few months with Steve's family), and I didn't know much about the business, but I was looking forward to my new position. I remember one ag story that stayed with me. Literally. I was assigned to visit a hog confinement and write about how the process of raising hogs has evolved.

As you probably already know, hog confinements differ from hog lots in that they're kept very clean—no mud or hog manure to gingerly step around. Even so, I smelled to high heaven after the interview. Instead of inflicting myself on the newsroom staff, I went home, showered, washed my hair, and changed my clothes before returning to the office.

Fortunately for me, the staff, and the readers, I didn't stay in the ag position long.

After a few months, I was offered the position of Lifestyles Editor, my dream job. As at the *Early News*, I didn't mind that I wasn't covering hard news. I enjoyed the softer stories. I met and got to know some remarkable residents by listening to them tell their stories. Some stories were heartbreaking, many were heartwarming, and all were stories that needed to be told. I'll share more about those special people and their stories in another chapter.

Back to my computer experience, or lack thereof. I had never used a computer before I began working at the *Reporter*. At *The Early News,* I had always written my stories longhand in pencil and then typed them on a typewriter. A typesetter in composition took over from there.

This blue Selectric typewriter is like the one I used at The Early News.

Psychologists say three of the most stressful events in a person's life are moving to a new location, changing jobs, and having a baby. After doing all three more than once, I would put *learning to use a computer* at the top of that list.

When learning to use a computer, one must first learn to speak "computerese." For example, an "index" or "table of contents" is called a "menu." An oval-shaped remote control is a "mouse." The little square on the screen that moves with the mouse is a "cursor," not "that little line on the screen that moves when you use the mouse."

Having played Pac-Man a few times with our kids, I knew a little about how those devices worked. I learned how to move up and down and sideways by hitting a key with the corresponding arrow. (Never mind that my children, even my 8-year-old, beat me every time.)

And so, with that tech experience under my belt, I sat down confidently in front of the video display terminal, otherwise known back in the '80s as the VDT. It was an uphill battle after that.

I gave it my best effort, and then I begged and pleaded for my trusty blue IBM Selectric typewriter, to no avail. Once you enter the computer era, there's no turning back.

After working in the newsroom for several months, I began to feel more comfortable with the computer. I was amazed at how much easier it was to use than a typewriter for many functions, like correcting errors with a delete key instead of using a white correction ribbon or a bottle of White-Out.

It turns out that I wasn't the only one who thought I might never catch on. Others in the newsroom were underwhelmed at the speed with which I was acquiring computer skills. In my annual performance review, one of the editors and my (self-appointed) mentor wrote, "*I was pretty nervous at first about Mary's ability to handle the Community Calendar, but she mastered the job efficiently.*"

Seriously, Jane, THAT was what you were nervous about? Typing up the Community Calendar? You should have been worried about me word-processing a crucial front-page story and then accidentally deleting it.

Unfortunately, that very thing did happen a time or two, but I didn't tell Jane or anyone else in the newsroom—I just quietly re-typed it, muttering under my breath, "I'll never get it right! Never, never, never!" (Picture Don Music, the pianist on *The Muppets,* who repeated those lines while banging his head on the piano keyboard.)

Although I had expected that learning to use a computer would be challenging, I was sure that handling the phone was one machine I had mastered. Wrong.

It was my first Sunday afternoon on duty, and I was working alone. They told me Sundays were always quiet, and it was. For about an hour. And then the phone started ringing.

I was in the middle of taking an obituary from the funeral director over the phone when another line rang. We had one phone line at *The Early News* that didn't ring very often. The *Reporter* had five lines. I knew I should do something with the little red button, but I wasn't sure what.

I panicked, pushed a white button, and promptly cut off the funeral director. I called him back, apologized profusely, and—you guessed it—another line rang. I calmly asked him to please hold (again), then raced to a nearby desk, picked up that phone, took a message, and then scurried back to finish taking the obit.

I eventually learned I didn't have to run from desk to desk

when multiple phones rang. It was just a matter of pushing the right button. Technology is amazing, huh?

I wish I could say that it was just the technology I struggled with at my new job, but the most embarrassing faux pas during my first few days at the *Reporter* had nothing to do with machines.

I had been sorting through old newspapers and had newsprint all over my fingers, so I went down the hallway to the bathroom to wash my hands. I knew where it was because I saw it whenever I walked by to punch the time clock. However, I hadn't noticed the sign high above the door until I finished washing off the newsprint and stepped out.

Three days later, I worked up the nerve to ask where the **women's** bathroom was.

Our laptops now go wherever we go—even camping.

18
Just a Man and His Will to Survive

"Risin' up, back on the street,

Did my time, took my chances.

Went the distance now I'm back on my feet,

Just a man and his will to survive..."

~Lyrics to "Eye of the Tiger" by Survivor

"If I am offered the job, we will go," I promised Mary.

Early, Iowa, had been our home for nine years, and life was good for my little family in the early '80s. There were times when we were just keeping our heads above water financially, but we struggled on because life can be that way sometimes—just trying to survive. Yet now, it was, perhaps, too easy for me to be satisfied with what we had and where we were.

One of the many activities we enjoyed was traveling to visit family and friends and discover new places. Mary and I took out a loan on a used 1975 Dodge Street Van. It was an eye-catching orange, with chrome wheels and orange shag carpet on the floor and walls. The van had around 80,000 miles on the odometer, and we put another 30,000 miles on it before we traded it.

The van's gas mileage was abysmal, and the engine would flood in hot weather when I tried to start it. I had to pull the engine cover (the "doghouse") open inside the van and manually hold the choke open on the carburetor to get it running. Occasionally the engine would backfire inside the van.

We took a memorable family trip to Disney World in 1982. All five of us slept in the van at rest stops along the way. When we got to Disneyworld, we camped at Jellystone Campground, sleeping in the van while we were there. It felt more like an adventure than a hardship.

Mary's mom, Grandma Betty, was back in the U.S. from Saudi Arabia, where she had worked as a nurse. She was renting a condo in Perdido Key, Florida, so we stopped and spent a few days with her on the way home. It was a wonderful vacation on a small budget. I remember thinking we had everything we wanted or needed.

Once again, it was a phone call that changed everything. The superintendent of Spencer Schools called and offered me the position at Spencer Middle School. I said, "Yes".

I immediately began to have doubts about changing jobs. We had just completed the first full year in a brand-new school building after the school explosion in 1982, and we were about to complete another successful track season. Did I really want to change jobs when this one was going so well?

I felt a responsibility to tell the team about my decision. The day I accepted the position at Spencer, I gathered the girls together after track practice and told them I would be leaving Crestland. I thanked them for their effort and dedication.

This little team had worked so hard and had achieved much. Of course, the runners disliked the painful workouts of repeated pace work. I'm sure they rolled their eyeballs whenever they heard me say, "Pain is your friend. It lets you know when you are training well." (As if that's any encouragement when you're in pain.)

As I was talking to the girls, my voice started to catch. I looked into their faces, some damp with tears, and memories came flooding back. I remembered the songs the girls played on the track bus, like: "Let's Hear It for the Boy" from Footloose or "Morning Train" by Sheena Easton. I don't hear those songs often now, but I think of those bus trips with the team when I do.

Many times, this small team had come close to winning meets with only eleven or twelve girls, but they were never able to make it to the top. Each one had done everything they could. I was so proud of them when the following year, the year after I left, "my" 4x800 team was the state champion. Without me.

I regret that I didn't have the opportunity to get our football team together to thank them for their efforts the previous fall. We put them through a lot of work only to end football season 1 and 8.

It was truly a very difficult year for us all. Class sizes and the low number of boys in high school forced us to play with only 17 guys out for football in '84. Those teams fought hard to represent their school with great hearts, and I thank them for their effort.

Coaching football and girls track at Crestland was a highlight of my time there.

All the memories of students, friends, the community, and Crestland school were an encouragement for us on our quest to begin a new life and build new memories in Spencer.

The recession of the '80s caused a financial crisis for small agriculture in rural Iowa, and Spencer was also affected by the downturn. The packing plant had been sold in 1977, and though it was purchased by another company, it struggled to reopen, leaving 400 workers unemployed. There were many homes for sale in Spencer in the summer of 1985.

Even though it was a buyer's market, houses were significantly more expensive than in Early. Besides that, interest rates were sky-high, also an effect of the recession. Interest on our first house loan in Spencer was 11 percent on a 30-year fixed-rate mortgage.

Just a Man and His Will to Survive

We found a house we loved in a nice neighborhood and said goodbye to 203 Walnut in Early. It had been a good, safe place to begin raising our little ones. In the middle of July, we loaded a U-Haul and moved to Spencer. We had a few regrets but were excited all the same.

Living in Spencer was certainly different from Early. Although not a big city, it was significantly busier. We established a "Do-Not-Cross-Grand Avenue" rule for our kids. Grand Avenue is Highway 71 north and south through the middle of town and carries a lot of traffic. The rule was made for safety's sake. Unfortunately, many of the kids' friends lived west of Grand Avenue, nearer the YMCA, so we did a lot of kid hauling to the Y and friends' houses during those first years in Spencer.

Once we were settled, we discovered Spencer Community Theatre. I enjoy singing, and Mary encouraged me to try out for *The King and I* during the summer of '87. I had never been in a theatrical show, and I didn't know how auditions worked. So, I sang the way I usually sing and read loudly with expression, my normal voice for teaching.

The directors must have thought I knew what I was doing because this red-haired and freckle-faced guy was offered the part of the King of Siam. (No, I didn't shave my head Yule Brenner style. I made sure that was in my "contract.")

Theater became a family affair. Our kids and I were in several musicals, and Mary helped with publicity, costumes, and props. It fit well into our work and school schedules since SCT musicals were always in the summers.

I was only slightly nervous about being one of the leads in *The King and I* until I overheard the costume head tell another staff member, "Well, I just spent $3,000 on material for costumes." Suddenly, realizing the scale of the theater's investment stunned me, and my anxiety increased exponentially.

I didn't understand theater well enough to love it then. Perhaps it's best to dive into an experience without knowing how far over your head the experience might be.

Barb Ambrosius and I in my first stage show, "The King and I"

The lyrics that could best describe my first musical stage show were to a favorite pump-up song that was popular before Spencer High School football games, "The Eye of The Tiger:"

...Just a man and his will to survive.

19
Breaking Up is Hard to Do

We were settling in comfortably, happy with our new home, and becoming familiar with the Spencer community. The kids adjusted to the move quickly, Steve was enjoying teaching middle school science, and I had a job I loved as Lifestyles Editor for the *Spencer Daily Reporter*.

After struggling to use a computer instead of a typewriter, I was beginning to feel comfortable with the new technology. I became fluent in "computerese," mastered the phone system, learned how to layout and design my pages, and now I knew where the women's bathroom was. (Down the hall, just a few yards beyond the men's bathroom.)

As Lifestyles Editor, I chose my own topics, set up interviews, wrote the stories, and designed the Lifestyle pages. I'm not very artistic, so I was surprised that I enjoyed doing page layout and got to be pretty good at it. Maybe that's because back in the '80s, the pages were drawn up on paper. These days, all layout is done using a computer app.

We had a great newsroom staff: a sports reporter, two to three news reporters, a photographer, an editor, and later, two co-editors. They were all excellent journalists, and I learned so much from them. I would have worked at the *Daily Reporter* for free—that is, if we hadn't had three hungry children to feed.

I also learned from the people I interviewed. They're lessons that have stayed with me even now, 40 years later. Here's a sampling:

I learned about dying with dignity from a hospice patient and her family, and I gained great respect for hospice workers. Forty years later, our family would learn firsthand how hospice care can help make a sad and stressful time a little less so for patients and families.

I gained insight from a young mother who told me about the challenges and rewards of having a child with disabilities with an uncertain life expectancy. I learned that one of the worst things you can say to parents in her situation, even if said with the best intentions, is: "God must think you're very strong to give you a child like yours." She and I would become co-workers and friends a few years later.

A woman whose husband was awaiting a heart transplant taught me about the stress that comes with knowing your husband will die without a transplant and the hope that a heart will be found soon. He finally received a heart transplant just in time, and I wrote that story, too.

The wife of a man with severe head injuries shared with me how his injuries had affected not only his life but hers and their children's.

I was touched by how the community gathered to support and spearhead fundraisers for a middle school student with terminal cancer. The same encouragement was given to a 19-year-old with leukemia. I happened across the leukemia patient's wedding photo in *The Reporter* two years after that interview. Unlike many of the people with serious medical conditions I wrote stories about, he survived.

Not all the stories were sad ones. All were interesting, and many were inspiring.

A group of adult students in a literacy course shared their stories about being unable to read and what motivated them to learn to read. One man told me about crashing his car into a river. He had seen a warning sign just before the bridge but couldn't read the words. After getting out of his car and walking back to the road, he stared at the sign and memorized the words: **Bridge Out.**

A woman who said she was psychic called me asking if I'd write about a support group she and a friend were starting for other psychics. When I interviewed the two women, they told me about seeing ghosts, knowing who was calling before the phone rang, and communicating with relatives who had died long before.

I'll never forget an interview I did in the spring of 1987, soon after the movie "Platoon" was released. Mental health professionals said that Vietnam veterans and non-veterans alike were experiencing increased depression and anxiety after seeing the movie and were turning to professionals for counseling.

I interviewed three Spencer veterans, all with diverse duties in the war. One served as a platoon sergeant, one as a medic, working in U.S. hospitals where drug-addicted military members were sent to detox, and one as a military policeman who later served as a criminal investigator for the Army.

The interview included all three vets in the room at the same time, generating a conversation between the men that lasted two hours and held me transfixed. Listening to them tell their stories was a fascinating and eye-opening experience for me and, perhaps, therapeutic for the veterans.

After arriving in Vietnam, the platoon sergeant said that his first assignment was to load bodies on a plane to send them back home. He was shot twice in combat. Even so, he shared memories of Vietnam's beautiful scenery and the friendly people he met there.

The medic had marched in Washington, D.C., with other college students protesting the war. He had been deferred once to finish college, and his draft lottery number was 16, ensuring he would be drafted. His options to avoid the war were to go to jail or leave the country. Instead, he enlisted and was told he'd be stationed in Germany. Nine months after demonstrating, he landed in Da Nang.

The military policeman's job as a criminal investigator included looking into drug offenses, shooting incidents, larcenies, and preparing cases for court martial.

Like most Vietnam veterans, none of the three got a hero's welcome when they returned home. They all hoped that watching "Platoon" would help veterans suffering from PTSD and allow non-vets to see the war from the perspective of those who fought in Vietnam. I wrote a three-part series from one interview, which won an Associated Press award.

Writing stories that fascinated me, doing layout and design that brought out my artistic side, and working with such great journalists contributed to my love for my job.

But, as they say, "all good things must end..."

That happened when a new publisher bought *The Daily Reporter*. It's a safe bet that there will be major changes in the newsroom anytime a newspaper changes ownership. The new publisher was a businessman more interested in revenue than good journalism.

Soon after the new publisher took over, a mass exodus ensued. The co-editors resigned, and the photographer's position was eliminated shortly after. Over time, three reporters took other jobs, leaving me secure in my position but missing my co-workers and friends. It felt like a bad breakup.

I loved going to work at the *Reporter* each day, but it wasn't the same with all the sudden staff changes. I began looking for another job where I could use my writing skills.

I applied for a position as director of the Retired & Senior Volunteer Program. I knew about RSVP because I'd written stories about the service opportunities offered by the national program, and I was impressed with the volunteers' willingness to invest their time and skills to make a difference in their communities.

The position required writing experience: writing grants and reports to local, state, and federal government agencies; newsletters; requests to local organizations for funding; reports for advisory council members; and presentations to community groups.

I knew my lack of a degree could work against me, so when I interviewed, I emphasized my journalism experience and familiarity with the area from working at the *Reporter*.

And I waited a week. Then two weeks. By the third week, I began to think they had given the job to another candidate (perhaps someone with a degree?).

After four weeks, I was certain I would get a "Sorry, but" letter in the mail any day, and I started checking the classified ads again. As a last-ditch effort, I worked up the nerve to call the interviewer to ask if he'd filled the position. My hands were shaking when I heard his soft familiar voice say hello.

20
Swiftly Fly the Years

When we were married in 1971, Mary and I thought we were mature adults despite being a few weeks short of 20. We had the rest of our lives to grow, love, and enjoy our family. All the time in the world.

And we had all the answers right from the beginning, recognizing later that those answers were naive assumptions. Father Time is stealthy, subtly bringing change when we think life will be clear-cut, firm, and steady with everything exactly how we want life to be.

The angst most people feel when their birthday clocks hit 30 is created by our culture and supported by age jokes. One of my friends received a 30th birthday card that read: *You have the body of a 20-year-old. Give it back; you're getting it wrinkled!*

After reading the card and laughing, I checked the mirror and found that smile creases were starting to form around the corners of my mouth. (*You're So Vain!*)

A sure sign that a person is growing old is when they begin sentences with "I remember." But I remember the morning our oldest child Joey started his first day of kindergarten. I was on bus duty that day, and our freshly scrubbed, sweet, smiling little red-haired guy stood in line waiting for the bus to take him to the grade school in Nemaha, four miles away.

Of course, it is almost inevitable that some older, bigger hooligan would push a little at the back of the line making everyone else ahead of him stumble. My heart felt as if it was being ripped from my chest. How can I protect him when I'm four miles away? I quickly understood that I needed to trust people to do their jobs and take care of everyone's children. Easier said than done.

Seven years later, when Mary and I were 34, we arrived in Spencer ready for a new chapter in our lives. We were about to begin the middle school years with our family. We gradually learned throughout this time that our children's sense of values came as much from their relationships with their friends as from their parents.

It is unsettling to realize that you start to lose them at such a young age. Yet you want your children to grow to be wise and independent people who understand the world around them... Emphasis on the word "wise." How could it happen when the kids are still so young that we, as parents, start feeling dispensable?

Soon after moving to Spencer, the kids and their friends discovered basketball at the YMCA and quickly immersed themselves in athletics. They were excited to learn about the many activities there since they had been gym rats at Crestland School. Because I was a coach, our kids had access to basketballs and to the gym whenever I was there.
In '86, Joe started 7th grade and participated in many activities offered to middle school students. There were

productions at the community theater in the summer as well as with school sports and vocal music. Aaron and Laura generally followed the same pattern established by their brother. The middle school offered football, basketball, and track, along with vocal music and band.

Laura, Aaron, and Joey, 1983

We wanted our kids to be involved in these programs along with their classroom work because they also teach character values—hard work, learning to be the best they can be, and contributing to the team's success. In other words, a very well-rounded education.

Spencer had a highly respected educational reputation and an impressive extracurricular program in every area, from the arts to athletics. As our kids grew and entered high school, we were impressed that they chose to be involved in challenging programs and classes.

We were concerned the competition levels in all areas would be much higher than the small school they had attended a year earlier. And they were. From a coaching viewpoint, everything about the speed of the game of football was faster, and the competition was fiercer. There were many more students competing for everything—not only sports but also academics and the arts.

Despite my concerns, the boys participated in athletics—football, basketball, and tennis—at the highest level, along with being a part of outstanding speech, drama, music, and academic programs.

Laura also participated with her brothers in the same quality drama and speech programs, academics, and athletic programs at Spencer High School. She excelled in basketball as well as track and field events, putting the shot and throwing the discus in state-level competitions.

Side note: Once, while watching Laura throw the discus, my dad laughed and said loud enough for her to hear, "I've never seen such a thing!" That was so typical of my dad. He had never seen girls participate in track or field events before. Laura enjoyed stretching the perceptions of what girls could do.

We are grateful for and proud of all the work, effort, and dedication our kids put into their accomplishments. However, I am forced to ask, "How did they get this way?" Our children were good students, but we never had to tell them to finish their homework, study for a test, or urge them to try out for extracurricular activities.

I am not looking for an "'atta boy" or a pat on the back from other parents here. In fact, as far as I can tell, it was our kids, not us, who set high standards for themselves.

I remember when Aaron was up past midnight, studying for a test. I told him to put the math (trigonometry, I think) aside, go to bed, get some sleep, and "if you get a low score, you can blame me."

Mary reminded me of a time when Laura had been working for hours on analytic geometry homework. She told Laura to put the homework away and spend time with her friends. Joe and his siblings did homework between scenes and when they were offstage during rehearsals for a stage production.

We can't help being proud of these kids of ours who did so well and never were the cause of sleepless nights. (OK, some late nights because of a train going through town or not being able to read a non-digital clock without numbers.) It's not like we threatened them (much), bribed them, or lectured them (maybe a little). But we really can't take the credit. How did this happen?

In addition to school activities, there were social and family events: Fellowship of Christian Athletes meetings, church activities, and get-togethers with extended family. We are certain that all of these activities contributed to our children making good choices.

The kids had part-time jobs and, as you might expect, dates. I wonder how we found the time to fit so much into the short space of five years. And yet, our kids weren't as busy as our grandkids are today.

As the days sped by, it was suddenly the spring of '92. Joe was graduating from high school and would soon be off to college. His graduation was soon followed by Aaron's in '93 and Laura's in '95.

A beautiful song from *Fiddler on the Roof* is a poignant reminder of those days: ... "*I don't remember growing older. When did they? Sunrise, sunset... swiftly fly the days.*"

Regrets? I have a few. Though we loved our children, we didn't tell them we loved them often enough. And we didn't celebrate them enough—their accomplishments, character, happy personalities, growing faith, or the lack of anxiety they caused us. We had every reason to trust them and their choices completely.

I waited too long to say, "I am proud of you! I love you! Thank you!" That's what I wanted to hear from *my* dad.

But I never did.

Art print by Bryan Andreas, courtesy of StoryPeople, Decorah, IA.

21
It's Not Too Late to Turn Back Now

In my last chapter, I shared memories of my time at *The Daily Reporter* and some of the special people I met while working there. But time moves on, circumstances change, and I needed to find other employment, so I applied for what sounded like a position I would enjoy: director of a five-county volunteer program that encourages people 55 and older to be of service to their communities. The director position would allow me to use my writing skills as well as put into action my belief that volunteers can and should play an important role in meeting community needs.

Another perk of the position was that I'd be home at a normal time most days, unlike my *Daily Reporter* schedule. There I would work until 11 p.m. or later on days when I was responsible for "putting the paper to bed." Being home at 5 p.m. every day meant I could spend more time with my family and attend our kids' school activities without asking for time off.

As mentioned in Chapter 18, I applied and was given an interview, which I thought went well. But four weeks later, I still hadn't heard from the interviewer. When I couldn't take the suspense any longer, I worked up the nerve to dial the phone and call him.

As it turns out, he hadn't had time to review his interview notes and decide on a candidate. (I would later find out it was down to two people—me and a woman with a master's degree.) He said he'd get back to me soon. That same day, my soon-to-be supervisor called and offered me the job.

I learned an important lesson here: It sometimes pays to be bold, ask questions, and do something that makes you uncomfortable. In this case, making that phone call may have been part of the reason I got the job.

The Retired & Senior Volunteer Program (RSVP) is a national program that places volunteers with non-profit organizations and public agencies. Every RSVP is required to have a government agency, educational institution, or non-profit organization as a sponsor. The Northwest Iowa RSVP is sponsored by Iowa Lakes Community College. In addition to my position, there are five coordinators, one in each county, who do most of the recruiting and placing of volunteers.

Our program's emphasis areas included literacy, education, medical transportation, health, and wellness. One of the biggest needs in our five rural counties is transportation to medical appointments and other necessary trips, including the grocery store, pharmacy, and social service agencies, usually for people who don't have a car and/or don't have a driver's license.

One of our volunteer drivers told me about driving an older man to his doctor's office when he noticed the man was perspiring, having trouble breathing, and clutching his chest. The driver immediately changed direction and took him straight to the emergency room. The E.R. doctors told their patient he was having a heart attack and that the volunteer driver may have saved his life.

A popular RSVP program is the Pen Pal Program. Volunteers are paired with elementary school students to exchange letters with their third- or fourth-grade "pen pals." The goal is to improve the children's reading and writing skills and develop relationships with the older volunteers.

The ultimate goal is for participants to gain a better understanding of the two generations. At the end of the program, volunteers meet their young pen pal for the first time at a pen pal party hosted by the school. Hundreds of volunteers in the Northwest Iowa RSVP have served as pen pals over the past 35 years.

One of my favorite RSVP stories is of a volunteer who visited local nursing home residents. One of the residents he spent time with every week was an older woman with dementia. She was non-verbal, and he'd never seen her out of her wheelchair. The volunteer didn't know if the woman understood any part of their one-sided conversations, but he always spoke to her as if she did.

It was almost Christmas, the nursing home was festively decorated, and a staff member was playing carols on the piano. The pianist finished playing, and for a few moments, it was quiet. Then, to the shock of those around her, the woman got up from her wheelchair, walked across the room, sat at the piano, and began playing.

The volunteer was stunned as he listened to her beautiful

music. It made him realize that we often write off people with dementia, assuming no part of their mind is intact. He told me that hearing her play was like witnessing a miracle.

I could share many more stories about RSVP volunteers and their impact on their communities by making a difference in the lives of those they touch. Equally important, the volunteers' own lives are enriched: they have a reason to get out of the house, meet new people, try new things, and feel needed and useful.

I was happy at my new job. I had a great staff, and we enjoyed getting together for monthly meetings and sharing stories, challenges, and successes. Although I missed my co-workers at the *Reporter,* the co-editors and I have remained good friends over the past 35 years.

One of the many benefits of being an ILCC employee was that the college offered free tuition to employees. I took advantage of free tuition and registered for just enough classes to earn an Associate Degree. I passed the dreaded science classes I had avoided 20 years before, with the help of a tutor, my science-teacher husband.

Buena Vista University has a satellite center located at Iowa Lakes Community College in Spencer. The two schools have a sharing agreement, offering reduced rate tuition for ILCC employees. I'd already taken a few mass communications classes at BVU's main campus when we lived in Early, so transferring my associate degree from ILCC to BVU was simple. I was on my way to finally earning a bachelor's degree.

I was 37 when I started taking classes the second time around. I often brag that it only took me 23 years to get a 4-year degree! My mom, two of our kids, and Steve were there to see me graduate. Earning a bachelor's degree also meant I would be moved up on the college's pay scale.

Another lesson I learned: You're never too old to go to college and never too old to learn. Even if you're not interested in getting a degree, taking classes allows you to meet new people and open your mind to new ideas. If you're worried about the cost or the pressure to get good grades, keep in mind that every community college offers non-credit courses that are free or low-cost, and they provide tutors if needed.

Aaron, Steve, and Laura attended my graduation ceremony at Buena Vista College in Storm Lake, IA.

Another one of the perks of being an RSVP director was attending required annual conferences held in great locations all over the country: New Orleans, Atlanta, Washington, D.C., San Francisco, and New York City. Adding interest to my regular duties locally, I was named to the Iowa Commission on Volunteer Service by the governor, another learning opportunity I thoroughly enjoyed. The first person I met at my first meeting was First Lady Christie Vilsack, also a member of the commission.

I was also elected to serve on the Board of the National Association of RSVP Directors. Our job was to be the liaison between local programs and the national organization that oversees RSVP. This position also involved traveling to interesting places I'd never been to before: Portland, Los Angeles, and San Antonio.

I may never have visited these places if I hadn't changed careers. I gained a love of travel mostly because of my RSVP job, and now that we're retired, Steve and I spend much of our time traveling to new (and "old") places.

I stayed in my RSVP position for 28 years. I missed working for a newspaper, but not enough to give up the RSVP job.

Although we worked together just three years, Lori, Jane, and I have remained friends for the past 30-plus years.

A final lesson: Be open-minded to pursuing interests outside your planned career path. That might mean taking a job that's not in the field of your dreams. (A little unintended baseball reference there.)

It's Not Too Late to Turn Back Now

I tell my grandkids not to worry so much about or feel pressured to declare a major or decide on a career while still in high school or even later in life. According to the Bureau of Labor Statistics, the average person changes careers five times during their working years. I think the important thing is that both young and mature people look for a career that makes them happy, even though that might mean going back to college, moving to a new location, or taking a cut in pay.

I was lucky enough to have had just two careers and three jobs in my adult life, all of which I truly enjoyed. Although I had some doubts when making each of the changes, I would do it over again—but maybe make a few better choices. For one thing, I'd take the difficult classes when I was 18 or 19. I'd also work on boosting my self-confidence level.

I made another good choice when I was 65: I retired! At the time, I had no idea another (almost) full-time job was waiting for me in the wings...

Note: RSVP's name has changed since I retired; the program is now referred to as AmeriCorps Seniors, RSVP. The sponsor is still Iowa Lakes Community College, and the goals remain the same.

22
Come Fly with Me

"Where does the time go?"

"It seems like it was just yesterday when..."

"Time flies when you're having fun."

Those phrases are attempts to brush off the realization that our little ones are not little anymore. How could this happen so quickly?

Our lives were focused on raising, providing for, and enjoying our children in the '70s, '80s, and into the '90s. Beyond the basics of life, we wanted to give them experiences that would enrich and help them develop into well-rounded adults. Before we knew it, Mary and I had spent two decades together, celebrating our 20th anniversary in 1991.

In observance of our milestone, Mary's mom Betty gave us the gift of a 4-day, 3-night cruise to the Bahamas. Neither of us had been on a cruise ship before. We farmed out the kids with friends we trusted, knowing they would be happy and safe, and we set sail.

Going on a trip by ourselves was a big deal for us. Up to this point, the only time we'd left the kids overnight was a weekend away each year for the boys' state basketball tournament in Des Moines with two other couples. Before the cruise, I thought staying at a Holiday Inn and having breakfast at Perkins with friends was thrilling and more than a little decadent.

We would sail on The Big Red Boat, owned by the Disney Corporation. It was red but not all that big by today's standards. Still, we were impressed. We sailed out of Port Canaveral, Florida. The only security precaution was a check for drugs with a drug-sniffing dog that went up and down rows of suitcases and bags. (Times, they are a-changin.')

We left port in the late afternoon, enjoyed a night at sea, and were in Nassau when we woke up. I enjoyed "cruising" the ship itself and what seemed to be never-ending buffets on every deck, including an ice cream machine, which excited both of us.

When on land during the daytime, we went sightseeing, tried snorkeling, and rode on a glass-bottomed boat. The water was extremely clear. Our only anxious moment was a thunderstorm appearing a few miles away from us, producing a waterspout. Our Bahamian guide barely noticed. When the waterspout was pointed out to him, all he said was "Ya maaahhn," along with a calm shrug of his shoulders.

The nights at sea were gorgeous, with the stars brightly shining and seeing other cruise ships on the horizon. We did experience some rough seas during the last night, along with some motion sickness. But we managed to get some sleep despite the rocking and rolling.

It felt good to have our feet on solid ground when we arrived back at Port Canaveral. We grabbed our luggage, hailed a cab, and headed to the airport to catch our plane. After checking our bags, we made our way to the terminal gate, where we discovered that our tickets had been changed. But in a good way.

Mary's brother Mike, who worked for American Airlines, had changed our coach tickets to first class. We were treated to a full hot meal served on fine China with real (non-disposable) silverware. This surprise was the icing on the cake after a memorable first cruise. It was a wonderfully thoughtful gift from Betty and Mike to mark our first 20 years of marriage.

A year later, our children began leaving home to pursue their education and independently start productive lives. Joe went off to the University of South Dakota in Vermillion in 1992, and a year later, Aaron left home to attend Iowa State University in Ames. Only Laura remained at home to remind us that we were still full-time parents. Her brothers probably would say we spoiled her. I'm certain she would disagree.

November of 1993 brought us some bad news. Betty, who had been an enthusiastic supporter of her grandchildren's activities since moving to Spencer in the late '80s, received a cancer diagnosis. She would undergo radiation treatments at St. Luke's Hospital in Sioux City. The treatments would begin in late fall and continue through most of the winter.

As her only family members close by, we wanted to be Betty's support system as she worked through this difficult and scary time. Throughout the ordeal, Mary drove her mom to the radiation treatments, a 200-mile round trip, sometimes through blizzards on icy roads. To our great relief, the radiation was successful, and there were no signs of cancer a few months after her final treatment.

In 1995, Laura graduated from high school and enrolled in the art program at Iowa State University in Ames. Seeing our last child leave the nest and head out into the world was sad. As we walked away from her dorm, I remembered the many times I had walked her to sleep, swaying, bouncing, rocking, and singing with her on my arm in my usual football hold.

Sometimes, while trying to get Laura to sleep (with her not showing even the slightest interest), I would calculate how old I would be when she left home, and it would be quiet in the house for the first time in 22 years. What seemed far into the future on the day she was born was now a reality, and we knew we would certainly miss the sound of their laughter and the busyness of their schedules.

After she'd been at college for a while, Laura asked us if we had a hard time coping when our last child left home.

"Yes, we did," we said with big sad eyes. "We didn't fully adjust to you leaving until about the time you got to Early..." (Early is on the way to Ames, an hour's drive from Spencer.) We thought we were hilarious!

Truthfully, every time one of our kids went off to college, it was a big transition and a learning experience for us and our kids. It seemed too soon for our children to leave home, begin their own lives, and finally have the independence they craved. Those days were gone, and there was nothing more we could do other than to love them, pray for them, and put them in God's hands as they went out the door.

I recall telling our children (usually after coming home late from a date), "Soon, you will be on your own, making your own decisions." And now they were. "Swiftly fly the years..."

Leaving home to go to college is a big step, but getting

married is on a whole different level. Aaron and Nicole were married in '96, Joe and Nicole in '98, and Laura and Dave in 2000. At each of those three weddings, I saw "kids" so young and vulnerable. (Never mind that they were several years older than when Mary and I were married.) Had they considered and discussed together what might lie ahead for them: class and work schedules, debts they will accumulate, and responsibility for their homes and vehicles? And what other surprises, good and bad, might come along?

Laura, before her wedding in 2000, holding our first two grandchildren, Jack and Timothy, who were the ringbearers.

We couldn't have been more pleased with our children's choice of partners. We knew they were perfect for each other and, with God's support, they would grow and learn together.

When they faced challenges that life throws at them, they would have each other to get past the roadblocks together. With a prayer, a smile, and a deep sigh, we watched them drive away into their future.

There is much to be learned about marriage as it progresses and grows. You must "learn on the fly," as we coaches often tell athletes in football practice. Mary and I still wonder, "How did two kids, not even 20 years old, have three children, manage it all, and stay married for 52 years?"

We were involved parents, but we weren't hovering parents. We watched with pride as our children navigated through their young lives when given the freedom to make their own choices. And we discovered that having an empty nest can—and should—be fulfilling for parents, just as leaving home is rewarding for their children.

Kids leaving home, graduating from college, and getting married are "The Big Three," right?

Wrong!

23
The Things We Do for Love

As I write this, it's almost Christmas 2022. Although winter is my least favorite season, Christmas is, and always has been, my favorite holiday.

I have happy memories of celebrating Christmas as a child. My sister, brother, and I were usually given two gifts: one was clothing—pajamas, new shoes, or a winter coat—and the second was a toy or something from our wish lists. Almost as exciting was finding the stockings we'd left for Santa the night before filled with treats, and always with an apple or orange stuffed into the toe.

Our first Christmas together as a married couple was equally memorable. Steve and I were still in college, and we were renting a tiny apartment on the top floor of the home of one of our professors and family. He was an expert pianist, and every evening we could hear beautiful music coming from his baby grand downstairs and wafting up the open staircase.

I gave Steve a guitar that first Christmas. He was surprised and delighted, but he never learned to play it. Still, it looked nice as a decorative item in our living room. When we had children, we bought a piano so they could take lessons. (The piano got only slightly more use than the guitar.) We propped up the guitar against the piano, thinking the effect looked like something you'd see on the glossy pages of a fancy home decorating magazine.

Years later, we gave the mostly unused guitar to our son, Aaron, who was interested in learning to play. Aaron took the guitar to a music store where he had it appraised. The music guy took one look at it and said, "About all it's good for is to stand it up next to a piano for decoration."

We burst out in laughter when we heard the music guy's honest appraisal. What can I say? We didn't have much money when we were first married, not to mention I knew nothing about musical instruments. My gift choices improved as our financial situation improved. In 2003, I surprised Steve with tickets to the Orange Bowl in Miami, where his beloved Hawkeyes were playing.

Steve gave me an unfinished chest that first Christmas. He bought it unfinished because it was cheaper than finished, and we stained it ourselves. We had very few pieces of furniture of our own. The chest was perfect for storing the new linens given to us as wedding gifts. We still have that piece of furniture, and we still use it in our dining room for storing placemats and tablecloths. (Although to be honest, I'm thinking of moving it to a room where it doesn't stick out like a sore thumb or maybe sweet-talking Steve into painting it.)

Fast forward 30 years. Our children were just starting their own families, and we assumed their budgets were tight. We suggested a hand-made/homemade low-cost/no-cost Christmas gift exchange instead of everyone buying a gift for each family member.

Laura, a talented photographer, and Dave have given us a variety of photo gifts: framed pictures, photo albums, photo pillows, memory books, and mouse pads with a picture of our family printed on them. Steve and I would probably have only a handful of good-quality pictures of our family without their photo gifts.

The kids have made several hand-crafted items, such as tree ornaments and decorations. Some of our favorite ornaments are little handprints our grandchildren pressed into clay and hung on the tree by a ribbon.

Joe and Nicole designed t-shirts with a bicycle logo and the names of each family member on the front. The bike theme has a special meaning for our family because we take an annual biking trip to Lanesboro, MN, together. Another time, they gave each of the grandchildren a week of summer camp at their house. (A very generous and brave gift—10 little kids to entertain for several days!) To top it off, they took many pictures and turned them into a photo album for each cousin.

Aaron and Nicole made a CD of favorite songs for everyone to enjoy. Another year, Aaron made brightly colored step stools. We use ours almost daily to access our loft closet, where we store Christmas decorations, memorabilia, wrapping paper, and miscellaneous but necessary items.

Our daughter and daughters-in-law are all excellent bakers. Handmade/homemade edible gifts have included loaves of bread tied with ribbons and jars of homemade jam on the side, a variety of Christmas cookies in decorative tins, and many other treats.

Our children continued to give us nice gifts in addition to the handmade/homemade gifts. At our age, we have everything we need and nearly everything we want, so we proposed changing how we celebrate the season. Rather than buying presents for us, we asked them to give a Gift of Love to someone else instead. The only guidelines were to find a way to give of themselves and involve their children.

That first Christmas Eve, we gathered around the Christmas tree, and a member of each of the three families took turns telling us about their "gifts of love."

When Joe and Nicole's children were young, they made and decorated Christmas cookie ornaments for residents at a local nursing home. The residents enjoyed having visitors and especially loved seeing the children and the edible ornaments.

Aaron and Nicole knew of a family in which both parents were in the National Guard. The mom had just returned from active duty, and the dad had been deployed to Iraq. The family committed to mowing the military family's lawn and shoveling their sidewalk for a year while the dad was overseas.

Dave and Laura's family knew of a single mom having difficulty making ends meet. They put together a care package of clothes, food, and toys and delivered it to the family just in time for Christmas.

We've continued that tradition every year, and we're always delighted and inspired by the time and thought that went into each gift of love. We no longer have the kids tell us the details of their love gifts, confident that showing kindness to others has become a family tradition and not just a once-a-year gift to us.

We've received many presents from our children over the years, but the best gift they've ever given us is the gift of grandchildren. We have ten grandkids born between 2000 and 2008—two girls and eight boys. They came in pairs: two boys a month apart, two girls a year apart, and two more boys ten months apart. One year, our daughter and both daughters-in-law announced they were expecting! Three baby boys were all born the following spring and summer within ten weeks of each other. (Our children are so competitive!)

Caleb, the youngest of the 10, brought up the rear in 2008. Although I tried to convince my children that he needed a same-age cousin, they declined to grant my request. But Caleb is happy to spend time with the next oldest three grandsons.

You can imagine what Christmas and other family gatherings were like at our house with ten little ones between the ages of 8 months and 9 years. Pure chaos! But it was joyous chaos.

As a grandmother of 10, just 10 days before Christmas, you might think I would be out frantically shopping or at least wrapping gifts instead of sitting in my sunroom typing and watching the snow falling gently outside.

Nope.

Christmas doesn't require (much) shopping for Steve and me anymore. In my next episode, I'll tell you about how we celebrate Christmas and create memories with the family—without the hassle and stress of finding the perfect gift.

As corny and cliché as it sounds: All we really want is for our children and grandchildren to be happy, healthy, and safe.

But above all, we pray they will show Jesus's love through the way they treat others—friends and strangers alike.

The grandkids with their stocking hats made by Grandma Betty

24
A Time to Every Purpose Under Heaven

As we close out another year, our thoughts turn to the new year ahead. But it's also a time to reflect on the year that has passed. There are days when we are anxious to put the past behind us, looking forward to a new beginning and a fresh start. But often, we are apprehensive about the future and what it may hold for us.

Never in my lifetime has the passing from one year into the next been discussed, feared, and caused so much panic as in the weeks and months before New Year's Eve 1999.

Many computers in homes and businesses still had older, less sophisticated computer chips and programming from the beginning of the computer age. The internal clocks of some critical computers were programmed to record dates with only the last two numbers of the year. Experts warned that 00 might be interpreted by some important computers as 1900 instead of 2000, possibly causing chaos in financial institutions, government agencies, power plants, and hospitals.

Some prognosticators predicted that planes might drop from the skies because of the effect the number 2000 might have on the computer function in airplanes and in the FAA's antiquated air traffic control computer system.

Millions of dollars were spent frantically developing software to prevent those disasters from happening. But the doomsday predictions proved mostly inaccurate, and the Year 2000 arrived with very few problems. We all breathed a sigh of relief.

There is a time for everything, the scriptures tell us, and we can do nothing to stop its relentless passing. So it was for Mary and me in the 1990s. Storm clouds were gathering around our extended family in the form of life-threatening health diagnoses.

Mary's brother Michael was diagnosed with AIDS in 1994. His treatment regimen kept him relatively healthy for a few years in the beginning, but as the disease progressed, the medicines were not as effective in the long term as we had hoped.

In 1998, my brother Tim was diagnosed with malignant melanoma. The skin cancer appeared as a flesh-colored growth which was unusual for melanoma. We usually think of melanoma as dark with irregular borders. Tim showed us where the doctor had taken out a big chunk of his upper arm. He said that his doctor had told him, "We got it all."

Tim had red hair and very light skin, and he was the most sun-sensitive member of our family, the one most likely to get severe sunburns. His nose and the top of his ears had scabs on them from the near-constant sun exposure that was a part of farm work in the summer, long periods of driving a tractor or baling hay. The diagnosis of skin cancer shouldn't have been completely surprising, but no one thinks bad things are going to happen to them or those they love.

In 1996, my dad Silas had a mild heart attack and five-bypass heart surgery. His recovery seemed to have gone well, but he never was quite the same after that. Dad would sit quietly at family gatherings without joining in on the conversation. It was as if he was in his own world.

My mom got into the habit of answering questions for him. Maybe his hearing was getting worse, or perhaps he was struggling cognitively and emotionally. We never could tell which. On at least one occasion, Dad got lost while he and Mom were driving in a town that should have been familiar to him. He had always done all the driving, but they didn't travel far from home after that.

Complications of AIDS took Michael on January 16th, 2001. We were able to be with him for his last days, along with Betty and his sister, Susan. When Mary and I arrived at Mike's apartment in Texas, he was heavily sedated. But when we walked into his apartment and he heard Mary talking, he opened his eyes and appeared to rally. Mike had recognized her voice. He seemed to understand that all of his family was finally together, and I think it brought him comfort and peace.

AIDS had left Mike weak, thin, and nearly blind. Over the previous three years, the disease ravaged the attractive and intelligent man Mike had been. That "Mike" had been taken from us—eroding away gradually with each one of those days.

We gathered around Mike's bed just before he died, joined

hands, and Mary asked me to pray on everyone's behalf. I put my hand on the bare skin of his chest to let him know that we were with him and that he could leave this earth knowing we loved him. A few minutes later, he was gone.

Michael Rosson McSwain 1953-2001

Our trip back to Iowa was quiet, both of us deep in our own thoughts. After a long 12-hour drive, it was a relief to be home. Even as we returned to our work routines, we continued to process Mike's passing.

We made plans to scatter his ashes on South Mountain overlooking the city of Phoenix later in the spring, as Mike had requested. Betty, Susan, and her husband, Dennis, would fly Phoenix with Mary and I for a private memorial service.

Along with the sadness at the beginning of the 2000s, we had some moments when the sun broke through the dark clouds. We were delighted at the birth of our first two grandsons right at the beginning of the century: Jack in February and

Tim in April, both born in 2000.

We celebrated the marriage of our daughter, Laura, to David Eckert in August of 2000. Our 6-month-old grandsons were ringbearers at the wedding, wearing baby tuxedos.

Another distraction from the sadness of the early 2000s was Spencer Community Theatre's production of the Broadway musical *Annie* in 2001. I was cast as Daddy Warbucks.

The Annie of our production was one of my middle school science girls. I enjoyed the special connection we had at rehearsals and school. I would occasionally sing, "The sun will come up tomorrow, bet your bottom dollar that tomorrow there'll be sun..." as she came into the classroom, and she would smile. That was her song, but it also seemed applicable to our lives at home.

My dad had a severe stroke in 1999, about three years after his heart attack. My 80-year-old mom, Doris, cared for him for three years until his death on February 6th, 2002. Though sad, Dad's death was a relief for him, Mom, and his family.

When a friend expressed her condolences to my mother and suggested that Mom would feel empty and alone now that Silas was gone, Mom replied, "The Silas I knew and loved left three years ago." She understood that there is more to a person than just their body and that a better life is still to come.

Mom was a woman of great strength and faith. "I will see him again in heaven," she had said. Not knowing how far into the future that would be, she lived another 14 years after Dad's death, but her faith was unwavering.

Tim's doctor's prediction that they'd "gotten it all" proved inaccurate. The melanoma had metastasized to his bladder

A Time to Every Purpose Under Heaven

and other organs. He died 12 days after Dad's death on February 18th, 2002.

Tim was a competitor, and he was strong-willed, like our dad, which put them at odds a few times. On his deathbed, though, when Sonjia, Tim's wife, told him our dad had died, he cried. Despite the sometimes-heated exchanges they'd had over the years, Tim loved his father.

Tim and Sonjia were at our house for a Thanksgiving gathering in 2001. It would be Tim's last Thanksgiving. All our family members were able to be there, my siblings and most of their children and grandchildren. Everyone brought mountains of food and desserts. How wonderful to be all together one final time.

Sonjia later related that, as they were driving away that evening, Tim looked back toward our house and said, "Do they know how much I love them?"

How precious it would have been to hear him speak those words directly to us. "Love" was a word we rarely heard in our family. Except in church.

In the days between Dad's death and Tim's, another ray of sunshine came into our lives in the form of a newborn little girl. Our first granddaughter and third grandchild, Allison Kathleen, was born on Feb. 15th. Her arrival was perfectly timed, our own little miracle restoring our joy and hope just when we needed it most.

> *To everything, there is a season*
> *And a time to every purpose under heaven.*
> *A time to be born and a time to die.*
> *A time to weep and a time to laugh.*
> *A time to mourn and a time to dance...*
>
> -*Ecclesiastes 3:1-4*

Jack, Tim, and Allison

25
You Are the Sunshine of Our Lives

When our family of 18 gathered for the holidays with ten little ones, it was a crazy, noisy, and, above all, happy affair. After opening presents, our house looked like a cyclone had ripped through the interior—gift wrapping, ribbons, tissue paper, diaper bags, toys, and sippy cups were scattered everywhere.

As the grandbabies became toddlers and preschoolers, it was clear to us that they didn't need more toys, clothes, sports equipment, or even books. Steve and I put our heads together and devised a new idea for the grandkids in lieu of gifts: Adventures with Grandma and Grandpa. The adventures would involve spending a day with two or three similarly aged cousins, doing something we were sure they would enjoy.

We knew the youngest ones might not understand why there wasn't a wrapped package from us under the tree for them to open on Christmas. And waiting for several weeks or months until the actual adventure was scheduled might be a hard concept for the little ones to grasp.

So, we decided to give the grandkids "clue gifts." We looked for inexpensive presents to help them guess what their adventure might be. The guessing game added to the fun for the kids and entertained the adults.

For example, the first year's adventure for Benjamin, Trevor, and Rowan was a trip to the zoo. (The youngest, Caleb, was just a baby—he would join his cousins the next year for his first adventure.) We gave the boys large stuffed zoo animals for their clue gifts. When our oldest grandchild, Jack, saw their clue gifts, he turned to us and asked, with a touch of indignation in his tone: *You're taking them on a safari?*

No, Jack. Grandma and Grandpa aren't flying three 4-year-olds halfway around the world to experience an African safari. Good guess, though.

Another year, we took Anna and Ally to a Build-A-Bear Workshop where they "built" their custom stuffed bears. Afterward, we spent some time window shopping at the mall.

When the girls were a little older, we gave them a "baking experience." We asked a local woman known for her beautifully decorated baked goods to come to our house to teach our granddaughters the fine art of decorating fancy cookies.

Anna and Ally had both enjoyed *Little House on the Prairie* books, so one year, we took them to the Laura Ingalls Wilder Family Festival in Walnut Grove, Minnesota, the setting for many of Wilder's books. Their clue gifts? Adorable pioneer dresses and bonnets that they wore to the event.

We've gone biking and camping with all of the grandkids. We took the two oldest, Jack and Tim, on a camping trip when they were about seven. As soon as we reached the campground by a lake, they couldn't wait to get out their poles and start reeling in big fish. After about an hour of watching patiently for their lines to jerk and not getting even a nibble, they started to feel bummed. Just then, a guy along the bank not far from the boys pulled in a large fish. I thought his success would encourage the boys to keep trying, but instead, Jack said dejectedly: "I think that guy got the last one!"

Other adventures have been a day at a waterpark or an amusement park, taking in a movie, touring museums and science centers, and riding on a train, followed by dinner out.

As the grandkids got older, the gifts got more sophisticated (and more expensive, as you might guess). Instead of the usual one-day events, the adventures became overnighters. We took the kids to Broadway musicals and concerts—events that Steve and I have always enjoyed. We hoped to cultivate their interest in music and drama while also spending quality time with the grandkids. It worked. We can't take all the credit for their involvement in theater and music—their parents also enjoy Broadway shows.

We planned an overnight astronomy adventure for the four youngest boys, staying in a cabin built out of a grain bin. It was at a county park near Steve's family's homeplace, where they could fish, explore, and look at the night sky through their telescopes (clue gifts for this adventure). And, of course, they got an astronomy lesson from Grandpa Steve, a retired science teacher, who pointed out a new comet recently identified by astronomers.

We also took the grandchildren to the Hot Air Balloon Races in Indianola, IA, Science Centers with IMAX Theaters in

Des Moines and St. Paul, Lego Land at Mall of America, and a Globe Trotters game in Cedar Rapids. After the main event, we usually go to a restaurant of their choice and stay at a hotel with a swimming pool.

Once the grandkids graduated from high school, we realized it would be more difficult to plan adventures with them—especially since they'd be living in different cities to attend colleges with varied holiday schedules. So, we decided to do one last "Big Adventure" after graduation.

For Jack and Tim's Big Adventure, we flew with them to New York City. We spent a few nights in a Times Square hotel and went to the Broadway show, *Hadestown*. Their first clue gift was a big red apple. We thought that might stump them, that it was too random, but they guessed NYC as soon as they opened the gift bag. (A follow-up clue, which, as it turned out, wasn't necessary, was a *Hadestown* t-shirt.)

We flew Anna and Ally to Orange Beach, Alabama, in 2021 after they graduated from high school. Steve and I have rented a condo there every winter. We walked on the beach, took the girls to our favorite sites and restaurants, and got great photos at The Yard ice cream shop. Their clue gifts were beach towels and T-shirts from Orange Beach.

This year, 2022, it's Charlie's and Sam's turn for their Big Adventure. I can't tell you what it is because I don't want to spoil the surprise (on the off chance they might be reading this). They'll find out when they open their "clue gifts" at our family Christmas get-together.

We try to remember to take plenty of pictures at every adventure and then have copies made to put in photo albums which we give to the grandkids at Christmas. We are surprised at how much they enjoy looking through those photos and remembering our adventures together from the previous year.

The adventures have been a successful experiment. Not only do the grandchildren look forward to spending time with their cousins and grandparents, but Steve and I benefit as well. Even though we have to come up with clue gifts, we spend far less time shopping, looking for the perfect presents. More importantly, the adventures give us quality time with the grandkids two- or four-on-two instead of two-on-10.

We're not touting our adventure idea as being original. I'm sure we got the idea from someone else or read it somewhere. But we're always pleased when we hear of other grandparents we know, many of whom are good friends, doing the same. We know many grandparents have adventures with their grandkids all year—they just don't call them Christmas gifts. And that's great, too.

You might point out that we're still commercializing Christmas by spending money on adventures, and maybe that's true. However, adventures can be done on any budget. They don't need to cost a lot. In fact, I think they'd say that being with their cousins—and hopefully, their grandparents, too—is their favorite part of the adventures.

I'd also like to think that all of our children and grandchildren would be just as happy to spend time together as a family without any gifts or adventures. And I am certain they believe that Christmas is not about the gifts under the tree, and it's not just one day out of the year.

I've always appreciated this quote from Mother Theresa that sums up perfectly how I feel about Christmas:

It's Christmas every time you let God love others through you. Yes, it is Christmas every time you smile at your brother and offer him your hand.

The grandchildren in birth order on a slide at Cedar Valley Resort. From top: Jack, Tim, Ally, Sam, Anna, Charlie, Benjamin, Trevor, Rowan, and Caleb.

You Are the Sunshine of Our Lives

Ally and Anna ordered giant sundaes with Grandpa Steve while on their "big adventure" to Orange Beach.

*The four "little boys" pose at the zoo.
Well, three of them are posing; Caleb appears to be distracted.*

26
The Sounds of Music

When Mary first asked me to co-author Kindle Vella episodes that would later be published as a book, I was reluctant and puzzled. Mary is the writer of the family. I am an average writer at best.

I found the idea appealing enough to say yes because I simply enjoy recalling memories from my past. I love sharing stories about how life used to be—ordered and uncomplicated. At least, that's the way it seemed at the time.

We are now about halfway through our book, and I am surprised by the clarity this project has brought for me. Writing this memoir is like therapy on a small scale. It has forced me to question my previously held stereotypes, confront my sometimes inaccurate assumptions, and better understand my family's dynamics. I know more honestly who I am since putting my thoughts on paper. I realize what is

The Sounds of Music

important in my life and am more able to understand what got me to this point over the last 70 years.

As I've mentioned, I was the youngest in the Steele family consisting of two sisters, Sue and Virginia, followed by four boys: Phil, Tim, Tom, and me. All were two years apart except for me, the tailender. I was four years behind Tom.

We boys considered ourselves to be athletes even when we were in grade school. Our dad was a star football player and track sprinter at his high school in Sutherland, and we wanted to be like him. We were strong, rough, and rugged farm boys. Football was the main sport in which we expected to excel.

My mother had another plan for her children. While she didn't object to our playing football and other sports, Mom had decided that music should also be an important part of our development.

All six of us played instruments in the school band. Virginia played French horn, Sue and Tim played trombone, and Phil and Tom played trumpet. As the youngest, I wanted to be different, so I chose the baritone horn. We all played in the concert and marching bands and sang in the concert choir. Sutherland Schools had a strong music program, considering it had only about 45-50 students per class.

Mom had shared stories with us about her mother, Laura (for whom our daughter was named), who had a passion for vocal and instrumental music which was passed on to her children. Mom and her sisters sang and played piano. Their brother Wayne also had a beautiful baritone voice.

My grandparents owned a piano that was hauled from one farm to another in their many moves during Mom's childhood. She and I sat in front of that same piano while she tried to teach me to play. I learned a few simple songs and felt genuinely good about that small accomplishment.

However, the call of the outdoors for this farm boy ended up being the stronger influence, though I regret to this day not continuing piano lessons.

I knew I could sing well when I was quite young. I first started singing Sunday School songs and hymns in church. I sang the melody but would also listen to my mom when she sang the alto part. My mother had a beautiful, mellow alto voice, and I wanted to sing harmony like her. I could also hear my older brothers singing bass and tenor parts. I wanted to sound like them, too, but I couldn't hit the low notes. I could sing the high tenor notes with confidence, and to be honest, any 8-year-old boy can sing soprano if he wants to.

When I was in 4th grade, the music teacher chose me to sing a small solo in a Christmas operetta, which helped me realize I could do something well that was a bit unusual for kids my age. Because of that, I considered myself something of a prodigy.

The Steele Brothers Quartet was formed when Mom found a book of church songs arranged for a male quartet. Mom accompanied us on the piano. Phil sang bass, Tim, baritone, Tom, second tenor, and I sang first tenor. I was only nine, so I could easily reach the high notes. I was hooked.

The Steele Brothers provided music for our church on Sunday mornings and evenings and sang for other churches in the area having revival meetings and youth group rallies for a couple of years. We sounded pretty good and gained a small bit of fame in the churches around my hometown. People I had never met knew who I was, making me feel a little famous (if only briefly). I was almost 11 and felt like "somebody" for the first time.

The Sounds of Music

Although we enjoyed music, football and other athletics were still our priorities. We four aspiring but average young athletes worked hard on the playing field to help give our teams a chance to win. We weren't stars, we were just part of the team, working together for success, but there is a feeling of excellence when a team is all pulling together. It felt good.

The Steele Brothers Quartet gave their final performance for their parents' 50th-anniversary celebration. From left: Steve, Tom, Tim, and Phil.

But teamwork is important in music as well. We boys practiced our parts so that together we'd be the best we could be. It was surprising to us, at least to me, that the Steele boys would be known and remembered not only for a very good sound but for sharing faith through music. It wasn't football, but it did require working together as a team.

I liked high school, although I was not a great student. I especially enjoyed the social aspect of school, and I loved science and physical education. I also enjoyed history and literature but was never comfortable with math. I hated tests of any kind—I still do. Couldn't teachers just trust that I had learned everything I needed to know?

Regardless of how I was feeling during the school day, there was a bright spot every day, and that was music. Band and chorus were scheduled for alternate days, but it didn't matter whether I was playing my horn or singing. I always felt relaxed, revitalized, and refreshed after music periods.

Phys Ed and athletics fed my competitive side, which was powerful when trying to keep up with three older brothers. But along with competition comes a lot of stress and anxiety. Athletes are pitted against teammates to decide who is best and who will play the most. The team is expected to be victorious over the team from a neighboring town; the players are expected to beat someone or something.

Music was freeing for me, or maybe I didn't take it as seriously as athletics. I just enjoyed it.

When I left home for college, I still believed sports would be a part of my future. I enjoyed the challenge of athletics and the achievement of fitness and strength goals needed to compete well.

I received a small athletic scholarship for the community college, which helped financially, but the chance to participate didn't turn out as I'd hoped—the school decided to drop its football program. Instead, the music opportunities available to me at the Christian college would form and shape my life. I traveled to different states with singing groups representing the college which helped me feel comfortable sharing my faith through music.

Throughout all the changes in my life, the one constant has been music. I have found it challenging yet comforting. At times I can't believe the beauty of a melody or the depth of thought a poet put into forming the lyrics to a song. You may have noticed that I mention songs often in my writing. Those songs frequently play in my head as I go about my day.

I continue to play and sing when and where I can. I have sung in musicals at our community theater and concerts over the holidays. Occasionally I am asked to sing at funerals, which I consider a great honor.

In 2015, I bought an old baritone horn and started playing instrumental music again 46 years after high school, the last time I had picked up a baritone. The main opportunities to play now are for the Spencer Municipal Band in the summer and Tuba Christmas every December. I practice almost every night.

Playing baritone in the Spencer Municipal Band

There is something so special about a single chord played together on musical instruments by 40 people at the right moment, all in tune. It is thrilling. It is surely one of the most beautiful forms of teamwork I have ever had the privilege of which to be a part.

Our children picked up our love of musical theater. Here, Joe plays Aladdin in "Wishes."

27
Shower the People You Love with Love

We closed out 2022 in a whirlwind of activities, reunions, celebrations, and emotions. It was a busy time, a sad time, and a scary time. It was also a time of joy.

Our last week of the year went like this:

Tuesday all of our children and grandchildren, including our oldest grandson's new wife (19 in all), celebrated Christmas in our home.

Tuesday afternoon, while we were opening white elephant gifts, Steve's dermatologist called to tell him the growth on his neck that she had biopsied a few days earlier was melanoma. He would need to go to Sioux Falls, SD, to have it removed as soon as possible. We didn't share the news with our kids that day. Steve's brother died of melanoma, and we knew they would be worried. We didn't want to dampen everyone's holiday spirit.

Wednesday was our only day to pack and load the van for our trip south, where we would spend the next two months. (Who packs for a two-month trip in just one day? I wouldn't recommend it.)

Thursday Steve had the procedure to remove the malignant growth from his neck. We left the dermatology clinic with him sporting a large bandage covering a 2½-inch excision; the skin was pulled together with 12 stitches. We spent the night in La Crosse, WI.

Friday morning we drove to Viroqua, WI, where I was born, and 10 miles from Readstown where I spent my first 18 years. We made this side trip to attend a memorial service for my childhood pastor's wife, Bernice, a sweet woman who put others before herself. She'd lived a full life and died peacefully in her sleep at 99. Bernice had told her five sons that she was ready to meet Jesus and join loved ones who had gone on before her.

The service was more like a celebration than a funeral, reuniting family and friends and sharing memories. We were able to catch up with Bernice's sons, who were good friends from church, high school, and college, but we hadn't seen them in several years.

Saturday was New Year's Eve. We stopped overnight in Clarkesville, TN, where we had supper with my brother's daughter, Leslie, her husband, Steve, and their daughter, Makenzie. We only see them about once a year, so it's always nice to be together, even if it's not as often as we'd like. In between annual visits, we rely on keeping in touch through Facebook.

It was a quiet New Year's Eve for us. When I was younger, we stayed up late to usher in the new year. This year, we were in bed at 10:30 p.m.

There was a time when I wrote New Year's Resolutions. I don't anymore because my resolutions were almost identical from one year to the next (lose weight, eat more healthily, exercise, read more, and be kind to everyone I come in contact with). I have that list committed to memory, so it seems like a wasted effort to write it down every year. I try to keep my promises to myself, and I follow through successfully (to varying degrees).

All these events coming together in the same week made me pause for reflection: endings and beginnings, tears and laughter, anxiety and relief, life and death. The fact that I turned 71½ during those five days may have also influenced my desire to examine my life.

My mind flashed back to just after New Year's Day in 2009. My mom, Betty, was dying of cancer. My sister, Susan, and I cared for her during her last weeks. We relied heavily on hospice staff to keep Mom pain free and help prevent Susan and me from falling apart.

Reading the hospice materials taught me so much about death and dying that I hadn't known before. The most surprising finding was this:

The greatest fear of people who are dying is not the fear of pain, and it's not even the fear of death. It's the fear of being forgotten and that they didn't make a difference during their time on this earth.

It made me think about how quickly our lives fly by and how vulnerable we are as humans. I pondered how one small malignant growth the size of the head of a pin can grow quickly and threaten our lives, but also how the thing we call an ending opens up to a new start.

With each new year, we have another chance to put the old year behind us and start fresh with a clean slate. A new beginning.

How do we begin again?

Maybe start by telling the people we love how much they mean to us. Tell them **now** we love them—don't wait until they're nearing the end of *their* lives to share all the ways they made a difference in *our* lives.

Take time to reflect—not just on New Year's Eve but throughout the year. Ask ourselves regularly: What have I accomplished during my life? Have I had a positive impact on the world? Have I made any difference?

At age 71, I know my "best-when-used-by date" is getting closer. Keeping that in mind, I resolve to follow my own advice in 2023. I will pause more often to examine my life. I will evaluate how I can positively impact my family, friends, and even the world in some small way.

I don't know if Mom worried she'd be forgotten, but after she died, I wrote her story, *Betty: A Memoir*. The driving force behind publishing her life story was that I didn't want my children and grandchildren to forget Grandma Betty.

Mom's story continues to make a difference in the lives of other people: single moms raising their children alone on a tight budget; adult children dealing with the grief of losing a parent or loved one; nurses and hospice workers who were reminded how much patients and their families appreciate them.

Betty: A Memoir, my first book.

I like how Ralph Waldo Emerson sums up his thoughts on the reason for living:

The purpose of life is not to be happy. It is to be useful, to be honorable, to be compassionate, to have it make some difference that you have lived and lived well.

At the risk of sounding presumptuous, I'd like to add to Emerson's quote: If we strive to be useful, honorable, and compassionate, we will also be happy.

Oh, and Steve? His dermatologist told him he has the "best" type of melanoma, which usually involves only the epidermis and rarely metastasizes. It also helps that the malignancy was caught early because Steve diligently checks for suspicious signs and sees his dermatologist every six months. With that prognosis, we feel he has a new lease on life. A new beginning.

Happy New Year, everyone! Begin again and make this your best year ever.

28
Keeps Me Searching for a Heart of Gold

How do you cope in difficult times? It helps me to have caring family and friends. Their encouragement flows subtly, often with a patient nod or a listening ear. Sometimes, their support is more direct, "Come over for coffee, and let's talk."

The people I worked with at school in 1976 were like that. We were a gaggle of young teachers and administrators who were all hired at about the same time. We were close in age—Mary and I were the youngest of the group. It was my first teaching position, I was 25, and I felt like a rookie.

The first two years of teaching were challenging, but the staff grew up together, providing advice and leadership for one another. We all had young families and many conversations about raising kids, behavior issues, and finances.

Mary shared a conversation with me that she had with one of

our new friends back when we all had young children. Margo had two kids a little older than ours, just 11 months apart. On a particularly bad day, Mary asked, "With two children born so close together, how did you not go crazy when they were toddlers?"

Our friend replied, totally seriously: "Mary, there were days when I WAS crazy!"

The honesty of that admission made it easier for Mary and I to accept that neither our children nor our lives would be perfect. We knew there would be challenges. The difficulties we faced would be the same for all of us, and we knew our friends could be counted on for support. Although perhaps not perfect, the staff of our small school became close, like family.

Another friend, Millie, the principal's wife, watched our two preschoolers while Mary worked part-time at *The Early News*, her first job after having children. We never worried about our kids when they were with Millie.

We remained good friends with Margo and Millie and their husbands, Tom and John, even after they had taken positions at other schools and moved away. We were sad to see them go, but the bonds of friendship stretched to wherever they were living.

The three couples planned activities together to stay in touch—camping, biking, and frequent trips. We had an annual tradition of spending a weekend in March attending the state basketball tournaments in Des Moines.

It was a great comfort to have our friends' quiet support after the passing of Mary's brother, my brother, and my dad, all within a few months of each other. Many days, we felt the emptiness of the gaps they left in our family, so having special people allied with us was reassuring and appreciated.

In 2005, we scheduled a trip to Maui with those two couples. It was our first big trip together, the planning of which started a year in advance. A few weeks before we were to fly out, I saw my doctor for a required school physical. I shared with him that I had been having feelings of anxiousness occasionally, and I could sometimes feel my heart racing. I thought the stress of juggling everything teachers and coaches deal with could be the reason for my anxiety.

My doctor ordered an EKG and diagnosed atrial fibrillation. He immediately put me on two drugs, one to control my pulse rate and another, Warfarin, a blood thinner, to prevent blood clots. Because of the blood thinner, I would have to go to the clinic for blood tests every two weeks to verify that I was getting the correct dosage.

Though it wasn't a heart attack, it still wasn't great news. I didn't want to be saddled with pills and blood tests for the rest of my life, but I didn't want to have a stroke, either. I realized the news could have been much worse.

One of the activities I wanted to experience in Maui was a bike ride down Haleakala, the volcano that formed the east half of the island 750,000 years ago. The ride would be about 20 miles long, all the way to the coast.

I made the mistake of telling my doctor about my plan. He nixed the idea immediately. He didn't want me crashing on my bike and bleeding out because of the blood thinner. I didn't tell him I was also planning a zipline adventure for fear he would give a thumbs down to that, too. (It was fantastic and educational!).

Mary and I also wanted to experience snorkeling while in

Maui. We looked forward to frolicking with sea turtles and watching angel fish up close in their own habitat. We made reservations for a guided three-hour snorkeling activity. Before getting into the kayaks, we were given much-needed training to help us gain confidence to experience a successful snorkeling adventure.

When we arrived at the beach on the island's south side, six kayaks were lined up neatly on the sand. Our leader gave instructions on how to use the snorkeling equipment, had us practice getting out of and back into the kayak while out on the ocean, and taught us how to paddle so we would stay close to the other kayaks in our group. But none of the training prepared us for the scale of what we were about to experience.

As beautiful as it was, we'd had enough after an hour and a half of rocking in the swells, looking into 60 feet of water with goggles that have curved lenses, and swallowing salt water. Seeing sea turtles, fish, and a bit of reef was colorful, but it was not the incredible experience we thought it would be.

Although we'd been looking forward to snorkeling in open water, it was a huge relief to be back on the beach, where we immediately laid down, hugging the sand until the seasickness subsided enough to walk to the car.

After coming home from Maui, I began to give more thought to my A-fib diagnosis. I didn't want to have a life-long reliance on medications. So, in the fall of 2005, my local doctor connected me with a cardiologist at the Heart Hospital of Sioux Falls, SD.

The cardiologists there tried three different procedures: stand-alone drug therapy, cardioversion (heart shock), and ablation (burning faulty rhythm cells inside the heart), all with the goal of putting my heart back into normal rhythm. None of them worked for me.

In the spring of 2006, I saw a cardiologist at Mayo Clinic in Rochester, Minnesota, for potential options. A full day of tests was scheduled to prepare for another, more cutting-edge, surgical treatment.

The plan was to go in through the aorta on the left side of my neck, down into the left atria, and then kill the offending rhythm cells. The death risk rate at that time was just under 10% from clots that formed during the procedure. While that number got my attention, I was ready to take the risk if it meant I could go off the drugs. Somehow, the thought of taking medication forever made me seem old.

At the end of the day, after the tests were completed, we consulted with the serious young cardiologist who would do the procedure. For the first 15 minutes of the appointment, we sat silently in his office while he read through several pages of test results.

Then, in a calm, reassuring voice, he shared that the procedure I hoped for "was not ready for prime time." It was meant for patients with A-fib cases that were more severe than mine. I was getting along well with the medication, and the procedure's risk (compared to the reward) was too high for a patient like myself. He could not recommend surgical intervention.

So, our question was answered with a straightforward, professional opinion. I was a little disappointed but mostly relieved. Learning more about the procedure convinced me that the inconvenience of taking pills was far better than the risk of the surgery.

After we left Mayo, Mary said she felt like a huge weight had been lifted off her shoulders and that she "couldn't get out of that place soon enough." We loaded our overnight bags and headed home instead of checking into a hotel for the surgery the next day as we had planned.

Our friends were happy to hear the news, too. As one friend succinctly put it, "Getting old sucks, but that's the way it is." He was right; I was being proud and a little vain. (I was 55 at the time. That's NOT old!)

In the summer of 2008, we rented a house with our "old" friends just outside of Grand Lake, Colorado, on the side of a mountain overlooking the lake.

We enjoyed the view of the mountains, cruised Grand Lake on a pontoon, and studied moose, osprey, and the behavior of hummingbirds at a feeder on our deck for ten days. Spending time in the beautiful Rockies with good friends was fulfilling and relaxing. I felt refreshed, rejuvenated, and emotionally ready for the upcoming school year.

At that time, I never dreamed that I would retire from teaching in less than a year. But sometimes, our carefully laid out plans are interrupted by the reality of life.

Tom and Margo Gates and John and Millie Mandernach with us in Maui

29
Before You Go

My last three chapters have been about Christmas and New Year's. They're special days for our family and likely for yours as well.

Today is not a holiday, but it is a special day. I am writing this episode on Jan. 12, 2023. Today marks 14 years since my mom died.

Or should I say "passed away?" Is that more scriptural? More spiritual?

How about "breathed her last" or "went to join the angels?" No, too dramatic.

"Expired?" Nope. Too medical, too technical. Sterile.

"Since we lost her?" That could be misinterpreted.

When talking about someone dying, I never know the best word or phrase to use. And yet, choosing just the right words when referring to death is far easier than writing about the process of dying and the emotional toll it takes on those left behind. You can probably relate if you've lost a family member.

I've done a lot of thinking and writing about my mom's death over the last 14 years. Writing is therapy for me. It's how I got through my grief and the unexpected anxiety that came with it. Both continued far longer than I thought was "normal."

I thought normal meant "getting over it" in six months. (Isn't that what the experts say?) When I realized I wasn't getting over it after six months, I generously gave myself another six months, thinking I'd surely return to normal in a year. I wasn't.

Mom and me at the Readstown, WI, all-school reunion, 2008

I have learned so much about death and grieving since Mom died. I know now that people experience the death of a loved one differently, that there's no perfect formula for dealing with loss, and there's no timetable for grief.

After my mom died, I wrote letters to her. I told her about the kids, grandchildren, work, and everyday activities. I shared everything I wished I'd told her when she was alive.

I also asked her questions in my letters—there was so much I didn't know about my mother. There were so many topics we hadn't talked about and so much of her history that never came up in conversation, probably because we didn't ask. I could have asked her during her last few weeks, but I didn't want to upset or tire her during her final days. So, I didn't. Now it's too late. I regret that.

Looking back now, I think Mom would have enjoyed talking about her growing-up years, her marriage to my dad, which didn't last long, and her nursing career. But she rarely talked about her past unless we asked. She had so many stories to tell that will never be told, and there is no one left who has the answers to all my questions. I missed my shot.

When I first started writing the letters, I didn't intend for anyone to see them. I didn't even tell my children I was writing to Mom after her battle with cancer had ended. I was afraid they might think I'd gone over the edge. (At least I didn't stamp them and take the letters to the post office!)

As the letters began to stack up, I started thinking that what I had written to Mom might be helpful for my children to read. I decided to add some information, like our family background, memories from my childhood, and my thoughts on growing up without a father. I put all the random letters and essays together in manuscript form to give to our children and grandchildren. It had become very important to me that they didn't forget Grandma Betty.

When our three adult children read what I thought was the finished manuscript, they said, "Mom, we think you should re-write Grandma's story for a wider audience."

I was surprised and flattered. However, it was not an easy decision to publish a memoir about my mom and me. I wasn't sure she would want details of her life to be made public, and Mom was no longer here to tell me, "NO WAY!" Was it fair for me to publish a book about her when she hadn't had a say in the matter?

But I also knew that Mom's story had the potential to help many people who were experiencing grief, loss, and anxiety. She was a nurse and always willing to help others in any way she could. In addition, I hoped the book would give hospice staff and all nurses the attention and praise they deserve.

Or was I just trying to justify revealing her private life by making myself believe it would "help other people?" I honestly don't know. I do know that the book continues to make a difference for readers in various ways. I hope those mourning a loved one learn a little from reading about what we did well, but also from what we wish we'd done differently.

Another decision I made that prompted me to publish was to use all proceeds from *Betty: A Memoir* for nursing scholarships in her memory. As a student who struggled financially, Mom would be pleased that she had a role in educating future nurses through the Betty McSwain Nursing Scholarships.

Betty was published in September 2020 and has sold more copies than I imagined. We have awarded six scholarships in two years, with more planned for as long as the book continues to sell.

Writing the book became an almost full-time job after I retired in 2016. Now that it's published, I spend most of my time promoting *Betty* and coauthoring this memoir with Steve, first published on Kindle Vella. Proceeds from "Times…" will also be used for nursing scholarships.

I've done book signings, library presentations, and book club talks. I write news releases and create posts for *Betty* on social media. Writing and editing *Times They Are A-Changin'*... has been enjoyable and satisfying. I am grateful to have these writing projects to use my time in a meaningful way.

A new challenge for me is learning how to write and post Facebook ads with images. It sounds easy enough, but I quickly discovered it's quite complicated. However, advertising has been worth the effort in terms of book sales, but more importantly, because of the responses I've gotten from readers, most of whom I've never met.

I recently used this quote in an ad for *Betty* that is running throughout the U.S.:

"When you lose someone you love, you must learn not to live without them, but to live with the memories they left behind." (Unknown)

To my surprise, many comments have been posted in response to the ad. Linda wrote:

"Today, my beautiful daughter would be 52 years old, but God took her home at 13. I think about her every day and night. I am thankful for all the wonderful memories we made and grateful to God that I will see her again."

Annemarie commented:

"Today, my first child would have celebrated his 41st birthday, but he's no longer here with me in body but in my heart forever."

I can't imagine the pain of losing a child, and yet so many people have lived through that nightmare. I hope Mom's story has helped them and other readers get through the day with mostly happy memories.

Despite all my research over the past decade on death, I still haven't come up with the right word for dying that doesn't sound so harsh.

Maybe I should have led with, "Today marks 14 years without my mom." That sounds better, but it doesn't really work because I still feel like my mom is with me.

This philosophical discussion between Piglet and Winnie the Pooh sums up dying as well as anything I've come across:

"How does one become a butterfly?" Pooh asked pensively.

"You must want to fly so much that you are willing to give up being a caterpillar," Piglet replied.

"You mean to die?' asked Pooh.

"Yes and no," he answered. "What looks like you will die, but what's really you will live on."

Well said, Piglet. Well said.

30
I Just Want to Celebrate

The average age at which teachers retire is 59, but for the rest of the country's workers, it's 63. I retired when I was 57, three months before my 58th birthday. That's six years earlier than most Americans and two years sooner than most teachers.

I enjoyed being a teacher and coach, finding great life satisfaction in the profession. By the end of the 2009 school year, I had taught for 33 years. Each year, I tried to maintain the ideals and goals of high-quality education, but there are factors that motivate teachers to move on.

My reasons for entering retirement included misplaced politics in and around education and how teacher performance was being evaluated. Teaching is challenging enough without these added roadblocks.

I was also experiencing hearing loss, and understanding students while interacting with them was getting increasingly difficult. Middle school students are usually more comfortable when the teacher is at the front of the room and less so when their teacher walks close to them while asking questions, even when the questions are well-meaning and friendly. Frankly, it was getting a little embarrassing, and I realized it was time for me to go.

After studying Iowa's retirement plan estimates, I learned that I could retire at the end of the school year in 2009. I talked with advisors and discussed it with Mary, and I decided to retire from middle school teaching.

On my last day, one of the school secretaries asked if I wanted to sign up for substitute teaching. "I will when I get bored," I replied, expecting I would eventually be looking for something to fill my time.

I have been retired for 14 years and have not yet filled out the paperwork to work as a substitute teacher, and I have yet to be bored. Because of that, I consider myself somewhat of an expert on the Art of Retirement.

Here's a list of reasons to retire, based on my research, along with my observations to help you sort the reality from the hype and perhaps enjoy some humor:

Ten Reasons to Retire (and the Reality of Retirement)

1. You can get up whenever you want to.

Reality: You would think so, wouldn't you? Not true, though! When your body is used to waking up at 5 a.m. for 40 or 50 years, your internal clock will determine when you get up. I discovered trying to stay in bed and go back to sleep doesn't feel like rest; it feels like work.

2. You have no rush hour traffic to contend with.

Reality: Are you just going to stay in the house for the rest of your life? Have you seen the rush hour traffic on Grand Avenue in Spencer, Iowa? The 8 a.m. traffic is BRUTAL!

3. You no longer have to deal with the jerks at the office.

Reality: Whoa—hold on there, mister/miss. Life is full of difficult people, and your "office" gets much bigger in retirement. So, you're going to have to learn to cope with them. "You can't live with them, and you can't shoot 'em," a trusted friend often says (although she's usually referring to husbands). Those difficult people are around (but mostly on social media). Might I recommend a few passages from the Sermon on the Mount?

4. Where you live doesn't have to be dictated by your employment.

Reality: True, but the heart often decides where you live. What would all the friends you've made do without you? You have made friends, right?

5. You have lots of time to do the household projects you have been putting off forever.

Reality: Well, you could, but take it from a born put-er-offer: "If it is still working after all this time, what's the rush?" Other similar bits of folk wisdom also apply here: "Never poke a sleeping dog," and "If it ain't broke, don't fix it." There's a connection in those old adages somewhere. (I'll find it. Maybe later.)

6. You can spend winter in Florida, Arizona, or Hawaii.

Reality: That's true if you manage well…or invest well. (How is Bitcoin doing these days?) Thirty below wind-chills in Iowa have a way of adjusting one's value system.

7. You get to set your own agenda.

Reality: Seriously? The retiree who said this must be single.

8. You have fewer headaches because life is simpler.

Reality: What does "simpler" mean? Less busy? Less complicated? Less challenging? Retired people sometimes say, "I had to get a job to get some rest!" It is common for retirees to be busier than they want, even while doing interesting things they love and believe in. Still looking for a simpler retirement life? Refer to #5.

9. You don't have to report to a boss.

Reality: Refer to #7.

10. You receive lots of advice, nice cards, and gifts.

Reality: True. At my retirement reception, a retired colleague shook my hand and offered this important advice, "Never pass up free food or a bathroom." Simple, realistic, useful, and straightforward.

One card mentioned, "With retirement, one day can blend into another, so just remember: Sunday is when the 'fat' paper comes." (You may have to be my age to get the humor...not many "youngsters" have a real newspaper delivered these days.)

Along with good advice, there were other encouraging cards and notes. A note from one of my former students said, "I loved coming into your room every day. You were the best teacher ever."

I loved coming into my room, too. Mary had helped me put

up wallpaper, a floor-to-ceiling picture of Earth from the space shuttle Challenger. The "best teacher ever" part almost made my heart explode. I was so moved by her words that I thanked her when we met again years later. I told her, "Your note pleased me because I know I was not always my best self every day."

She responded, "Oh, you were not as gruff as you think you were." I had to smile.

My children surprised me with a retirement gift that fulfilled a dream that I hadn't thought about in years. They gave me a stockcar racing experience at the Iowa Speedway in Newton. Car racing was something I had fantasized about as a boy. How did they know? Could it be because they had to sit through my racing days stories so many times and ooh and ahh over my racing trophy? (Trophy. Singular. To be fair, I only raced in one event.)

As I was growing up, I didn't like farm work, but I did enjoy driving the tractors and the mechanics of all the equipment. I watched Dad take a tractor engine apart, replace the cylinder sleeves and crankshaft bearings, and put the engine back together again. That's how I developed an interest in cars, engines, and basic auto mechanics.

My brothers and cousins bought Hot Rod magazines and discussed which cars and engine brands were the best. They discussed the latest drag races, NASCAR races, and the popular drivers of the '50s. I was a gearhead from the time I was a little kid.

Back to my racing gift. All my children and grandkids traveled to Newton, IA, to watch me drive one of the racecars there. (It was a Ford...not totally bad. A Dodge would have been my first choice, but thank heavens it wasn't a Chevy!).

Cashing in my gift from the kids: driving a race car.

Our grandchildren were all there to watch Grandpa Steve drive a racecar: Rowan, Trevor, Sam, Charlie, Jack, Tim, Benjamin, Anna, Ally, and Caleb.

First, I rode with an instructor for five laps and then drove it on my own for 10 laps, following the instructor in a car ahead of me. The G-forces in the turns and the acceleration in each straight almost squashed the air out of me.

Admittedly, I was not the fastest student ever, but I was going 100 mph on the straights, so not bad for a rookie. The legal release I was required to sign before I got in the car said I was personally responsible for "any and all damages that might occur" while driving the car. That weighed heavily on my mind and made me ease up on the accelerator early at every turn.

That dream-of-a-lifetime experience was exciting for me, but the thoughtfulness that went into the gift was the best retirement present of all. My children and I grew up together, and they pretty much know me. (Although, again, I wasn't my best self every day).

Although I've joked about it in this chapter, retirement has been a blessing. It has offered me the opportunity to evaluate and rebalance my life. I was able to visit my aging mother on a weekly basis and be there when she took her last breath. I recorded Mom sharing her history and telling family stories I had never heard before. My brother Tom and I rediscovered and deepened our relationship with each other and our mom in the years before she died at 96, and I will always be thankful for that.

There were many other retirement opportunities available to me. I was an adjunct instructor for six years, teaching an earth science class at Iowa Lakes Community College. For four years, I served on the Foster Care Review Board, which aims to safeguard the care of children in foster homes. I was involved in several service opportunities through RSVP, a volunteer program, such as tutoring and mentoring students.

I ride my bike almost every day, regardless of the weather. I spend a half hour each night playing my baritone and singing. And I discovered that I like putting puzzles together. Who knew? It was a surprise to me.

To those of you who think you might be bored in retirement, I would say you'll be bored only if you allow yourself to be. There is a new world out there waiting for you, and there are a million ways the world could use people like you. Go out and find them!

31
Sweet Home-Away-From-Home Alabama

Watch more sunsets together.

That was a promise Steve and I made long before we started thinking about retirement. It continues to be a goal for us now that we've both been retired for several years.

Steve retired in 2009, seven years before I did. I liked my job, I had good benefits, and I hadn't worked as many years as he had. So, it wasn't a sacrifice for me to hold off on retiring until I turned 65, when we'd both be eligible for Medicare.

The arrangement worked well for us. Steve did a great job of keeping the house picked up, buying groceries, running errands, and doing yard work. He even enjoyed (most of) those somewhat mundane duties while I continued to work.

Even before I finally retired in 2016, we decided we would

make the most of our golden years, staying active and healthy, and spending our children's inheritance, if need be. (Their response: "Go for it, Mom and Dad.")

Friends who retired before us had been going south for several years to stay warm until Iowa's frigid winters gave way to spring. Some couples we knew rented condos in Florida, some on the Gulf, and many in Arizona. It sounded like a great idea to us. Although I was raised in Wisconsin and Steve in Iowa, neither of us likes the cold, icy, windy weather of the Midwest.

In preparing for retirement, while I was enjoying a long Christmas break from work, we studied a map to find the closest beach from our front door. The winner: Corpus Christi, TX. We spent 12 days exploring that area as well as Padre Island. In 2012 and 2015, we visited friends and relatives in Phoenix and Scottsdale, driving home through rain and snow.

In January 2016, we took a little tour of Florida, driving down the west coast and stopping in various towns we knew to be popular winter destinations for retirees: Port Richey, Port Charlotte, Ft. Meyers, Homestead, Marathon, and Key West. Then we drove north up the east coast from Key West past Miami to Orlando and Cape Canaveral. From the Cape, we headed west toward the Gulf Coast, stopping at Apalachicola, Panama City Beach, Destin, Ft. Walton, and Pensacola. We finally headed west across the Florida/Alabama state line through Perdido Key and into Alabama.

After staying with friends in Orange Beach, AL, for several days, we knew that was where we wanted to be in January and February. It's not as warm as Central and South Florida, but the rental prices are lower, and we have gotten to know a group of snowbirds there. We've been going to the Gulf every winter since.

Sweet Home-Away-From-Home Alabama

We are in Orange Beach as I write this. The weather has been warmer than usual, in the 70s, and clear most days. Our condo is on the beach. It's nice but not fancy. All we really need is a view of the Gulf. Every day, we watch for dolphins swimming by in the morning and coming back in the late afternoon.

There are signs that say, "Please don't feed the birds from the balcony." In addition to the mess they leave, they can be quite aggressive. Once, when we were having a picnic on the beach, a seagull swooped down and plucked a sandwich right out of my hand before I realized what had happened.

If you ever decide to visit the Alabama Gulf Coast, I need to tell you that there is a bit of a learning curve, and some adaptation is required if you're from the Midwest. Here is some helpful information I've learned over the eight winters we've spent there that may assist you in successfully crossing the cultural divide.

As you might expect, Alabamans speak with a drawl, which I find pleasant to listen to. I've also discovered some interesting nuances regarding speech in general.

For example, in a professional setting like a doctor's office, we are referred to as "Miss Mary" and "Mister Steve." If they don't know our names, say a waitress at a restaurant or clerk at a store, we've been called Hon, Darlin,' and Baby by staff half our age. Some people might think it's condescending or even offensive, but I can't help but smile.

We enjoy the diversity of cultures in the area. A Mardi Gras parade is one of many events held in nearly every Gulf town. The parades are smaller than those in New Orleans but impressive, nevertheless. Hundreds of thousands of necklaces made of beads strung together in Mardi Gras colors—green, purple, and gold—are hurled from the elaborately decorated floats to the masses of onlookers lining the streets. The people riding the floats wear colorful, artfully created masks and ornate costumes.

It's a lot of fun, but I must warn you against getting too caught up in the Mardi Gras celebrations. Although it's tempting to pick up all those (free) necklaces, Moon Pies, and plastic toys, think again. Although you may be able to convince your grandchildren to eat the Moon Pies, what will you do with 50 lbs. of multi-colored beads when you go home to Iowa? I've heard that some nursing homes use the brightly colored beads for crafts and Bingo prizes, and some art teachers keep them on hand for student projects. I'm open to suggestions... Readers?

You'll want to try some of the many eating establishments while you're in the Orange Beach area. As you might expect, all serve great seafood, and many have a Gulf view. We enjoy Tacky Jacks, which lives up to its name, but their Garbage Nachos keep us coming back. We also like LuLu's in Gulf Shores. In fact, we've named our GPS voice "LuLu" in her honor. Lulu is the sister of the late Jimmy Buffet, a well-known singer, songwriter, and guitarist. He also owned the Margaritaville chain of restaurants.

You'll want to visit Flora-Bama (but maybe just once) for the unique "cultural" experience. It's about six miles from Orange Beach on the Florida/Alabama state line—thus its name—and looks like a mishmash of shacks haphazardly banged together into one huge multi-level, natural-sided structure. In its dark interior are several bars with five stages for live music, a restaurant, an oyster bar, a souvenir shop, and a beach bar called Bushwhackers.

Bingo is played daily in a massive open space, which doubles as the meeting place for a church, Worship on the Water, every Sunday. Hundreds of people attend the service. As a friend pointed out, you can pick up a mimosa at one of the bars on your way into the worship services if you're so inclined.

Most attendees wear blue jeans and t-shirts, some wear expensive-looking suits, and there are usually several homeless people standing on the edge of the audience. It is truly a diverse group that makes up the church, as I think Jesus meant for worship to be.

The Bra Room at Flora-Bama is probably the bar that draws the most lookers. Hundreds of bras are "donated" and hung from the ceiling. I'm not sure how they hang the bras way up on the high ceiling, but they're all taken down at the end of the year. "Re-decorating" starts with new bras beginning on New Year's Day.

Flora-Bama hosts annual events you won't want to miss (I say this with tongue in cheek), including the Interstate Mullet Throwing Contest, Polar Bear Dip, Memorial Day Bikini Contest, Bulls on the Beach (a rodeo with real bulls), and a Fishing Rodeo.

If bars, restaurants, and unique events aren't your thing, there are plenty of options in the Orange Beach/Gulf Shores area. You outdoorsy folks will love the trails, many of which wind through the sprawling and lovely Gulf State Park. Walking, running, and biking are all popular activities. While on the trails, watch for gopher tortoises, armadillos, eagles, and alligators. A bobcat crossed the trail in front of Steve last week while he was biking. I'm kind of glad I wasn't with him.

One last tip: If you plan to spend winters on the Gulf, I recommend brushing up on your Bingo, card playing, puzzling, and dominos skills. Before wintering in Orange Beach, Steve and I didn't do any of those things very often, but there is peer pressure to participate.

We were a little surprised to discover that we enjoy playing Hand & Foot, Shanghai, and the dominoes game, Mexican Train. I draw the line at Bingo, which takes place at almost any senior center in the area, along with various card games. (They take their games seriously and are so competitive!)

As we walk into our home-away-from-home and look out at the beautiful water, we feel like we want to stay here forever. But when Feb. 28th rolls around, the boxes are packed, the car is loaded, and we're ready to return home.

I'm convinced that being here two months out of the year is good for both my mental and physical health. Nothing is more soothing than sitting on the balcony at the end of the day, listening to the waves lapping against the shore, and drinking coffee with hazelnut creamer.

And watching the sunset. Of course.

Steve says drinking coffee while looking at the Gulf is good therapy.

Art Print by Bryan Andreas, courtesy of StoryPeople, Decorah, IA.

32

We Are the World: Meeting Memusi, Part 1

Two years into retirement, the thought, "What's next?" weighed heavily on my mind.

A local doctor, a friend, had told me about traveling to other countries with Volunteers in Medical Missions. He suggested I consider going with him on the next VIMM trip to Tanzania.

I'd never been on a mission trip before. The idea was both exciting and frightening. I didn't have any medical training except what I had learned in Anatomy and Physiology and from the athletic training classes I took in college. I didn't want just to watch the doctors and nurses work—I wanted to contribute.

Before making a decision, I needed to evaluate my motives. Was it just a trip for my experience? Entertainment? Was I just pretending to be a missionary?

I remembered the scripture from 1 John 3, verses 17 and 18: "If anyone has material possessions and sees a brother or sister in need but has no pity on them, how can the love of God be in that person? Dear children, let us not love with words or speech but with actions and in truth."

I have the opportunity to go. I must go.

The VIMM team members came from all over the country: Iowa, Minnesota, North Carolina, Tennessee, and Texas. We all flew into Atlanta, met at the gate, and introduced ourselves. It was good that we had two hours to get acquainted because we were scattered throughout the plane for the entire trip to Africa.

The flight from Minneapolis to Atlanta was three and a half hours; to Amsterdam was nine and one-half hours; and it was another nine and one-half hours to Kilimanjaro airport in Tanzania, for a total of 22 hours of flight time. I didn't sleep for a single minute of the entire flight. Between the adrenaline, anxiety, and the infernal dinging of the seat belt warning or pilot call bell, it was impossible for me to sleep.

One last team member, a nurse from England, had traveled on her own through Africa by bus to meet us in Arusha. At the end of our two weeks, she would extend her trip to climb Kilimanjaro with another group. I wished I had half her courage.

Tanzania is a beautiful country sitting atop the East Africa Ridge. Because the ridge is cracking open, there has been much volcanic activity. Mt. Kilimanjaro, the tallest mountain in Africa, is one of the resulting volcanoes that has formed. It towers over the countryside and is sometimes visible from Arusha. It reminded me of Mt. Rainier near Seattle, WA.

Mt. Meru is an ancient volcano on the east side of Arusha.

Our home base was a nice hotel—it was luxurious compared to the conditions in the rural areas around Arusha. I shared a room with two friends who are doctors. We had a relaxing view out over a garden of trees and plants.

The bathroom was respectable, with a tub, shower, sink, and fresh towels daily. We were told to use bottled water to brush our teeth and to keep our eyes and mouths closed while showering due to the questionable water quality. It was a bit unnerving. We talked about how easily habits can subconsciously take over, and without thinking, you rinse your mouth out during a shower.

My roommates both used a CPAP (breathing machine) for sleep apnea at night. As my son so accurately put it, "I'll bet it was like sleeping with Darth Vader." It was, only there were two of them! I hear that CPAPs now are much quieter than in the old days.

Our job was to set up medical centers at church buildings in communities outside Arusha. We would spend a full day in each town, attending to the medical needs of as many people as we had time and medications for. People would stand in line for hours, patiently waiting to be examined and to receive needed pharmaceuticals donated by drug companies. We distributed mostly over-the-counter medicines for pain, blood pressure, colds, allergies, and worms. There were also salves and ointments for skin conditions. None were addictive.

There was always a cluster of children around us wherever we went.

My function was to be a pharmacist of sorts, along with several nurses, counting and bagging pills to be distributed to patients after seeing the doctors. This requires reading and interpreting doctors' hand-written prescriptions, which can be challenging. However, being a former teacher who had interpreted middle school students' handwriting, it was well within my skill set.

Since the VIMM doctors on our team were not licensed in Tanzania, they were not legally permitted to do any major surgery. They only examined, diagnosed, and then referred patients to doctors and hospitals in the country.

In one extreme case, a local doctor supervised our doctors as they attempted a simple but potentially life-saving procedure. A man's tongue had a tumor big enough to make eating and breathing difficult. Treatment had been scheduled for him at the area hospital, but it was still months away. The VIMM doctors were able to remove it quickly. It reminded me of the healing of the lame and blind in the Book of Acts.

Because of the restrictions on the VIMM doctors, we could not do much for our patients other than ease their pain and discomfort for 30 days until their meds ran out. Discouraging for us all was the recognition that no matter the diagnoses, and even with referrals to a clinic or hospital, our patients probably would not follow up with further treatment because they could not afford it.

Much of the water for Arusha comes from untreated sources—surface water where animals and humans use the same water supply, so every person was given a worm pill. Clean water alone would significantly improve the health of Africans.

Another organization trying to improve living conditions in Tanzania is World Vision. Mary and I have sponsored children in Africa and other countries through World Vision for many years.

One of those children was a 13-year-old girl named Memusi. We first started sponsoring her when she was five years old. While planning for the Tanzania trip, we realized she lived near Arusha, where the VIMM work would be based. Mary said to me, "You should try to visit Memusi while you're there."

So, before leaving for Tanzania, I called World Vision to tell

We Are the World: Meeting Memusi, Part 1

them I would be in Arusha and would like to visit Memusi, if at all possible. The representatives were helpful and enthusiastic about making the visit happen. After two telephone exchanges in two days, they had set up my visit.

The Masai village where Memusi lived with her family was 60 miles out in the country. The World Vision staff had contacted the family and provided a vehicle, a driver, a guide, Julius, who would translate from English to Swahili, and a second translator. Three languages would be spoken during my visit: English, Swahili, and Masai, so a second translator was necessary to translate Swahili to Masai.

When I asked if I could take gifts to the family, a World Vision representative told me that gifts of food and clothing would show respect and goodwill. Our guide, Julius, knew exactly what to buy that would be helpful for Memusi's family and where to buy those items.

At 8:00 a.m. on the day of the visit, Julius and the driver picked me up at my hotel. We stopped first at the huge outdoor market in downtown Arusha. We found a place to park our truck amongst the throngs of people buying and selling.

When Julius opened his door, I assumed I would go with him with the cash to buy the gifts. He quickly grabbed my arm to stop me. I was not allowed out of the car, he said, partly for my safety but also because prices for the flour, coffee, salt, sugar, rice, and beans would double if they saw a "rich American" was going to make the purchase.

With our gifts loaded in the back of the truck, we slowly worked our way through the crowds. I asked the driver how he could drive through the impossibly thick crowds, and he replied, "Be patient, drive slowly but steadily, and make much noise." He raced his engine loudly, and it worked.

As we started the 90-minute trip to the Masai village, I chatted with Julius occasionally, but mostly I was lost in my thoughts. I was anxious; my heart felt like it was skipping beats. I was thinking about meeting Memusi's family and what I should say. They might be suspicious of this American who suddenly appears out of the blue. Who is this guy? What are his intentions?

The topography was a beautiful plain punctuated to the horizon with isolated mounds and cone-like hills. I should have been relaxed, but my jaw was clenched, and I had a knot in my stomach.

The truck stopped abruptly. I tried to calm myself, preparing for the worst. Flat tire? Did the engine die? What if we have to walk? Are there lions out there?

Julius jumped out of the truck. My heart was pounding inside my chest. What was happening?

33
We Are the Children: Meeting Memusi, Part 2

I would meet Memusi and her family very soon. As we drove across the vast Masai plains toward Memusi's village, I thought about how the next few hours might unfold. Our only communication over the previous eight years we'd had with her were brief notes and pictures forwarded through World Vision. I was extremely apprehensive about the visit. What if they thought of me as an "Ugly American?"

Suddenly, our driver slammed on the brakes of the Toyota truck we were traveling in. I thought we were about to hit something in the road, and I listened for the thud of an impact. My heart was racing inside my chest.

Julius, the World Vision guide who had arranged the trip, got out of the truck. I was aware that we were out in the middle of nowhere. I went around to the back of the pickup, thinking, "If we need to walk the rest of the way to the village, it could be a very long walk!"

I heard something moving in the tall grass next to the road. We were out in the plains where big cats, hyenas, and snakes could be lurking in the grass.

Instead, a Tanzanian man popped up out of the grass, carrying a cute brown goat whose legs were tied together with rope. Julius introduced me to the man as one of our two translators (and also a goat farmer). I hadn't known that a goat was included on the gift list for Memusi's family. The farmer nonchalantly tossed the goat into the truck bed, we all climbed into the pickup, and we were off again.

I spent the last 45 minutes of the drive thinking about how I would greet Memusi and her family when we arrived at their hut. I knew nothing about Masai traditions and customs. I didn't want to offend them or, even worse, make them think I considered myself superior to them in any way.

I asked Julius for some etiquette advice. He reminded me I was a stranger to them, so when I was introduced, I should shake hands only—no hugs. But be friendly, he said.

When we drove up to the hut, I saw Memusi off to the side of the driveway next to her donkey, on which were tied large plastic water jugs. One of her daily tasks was to take the donkey to get water. The village's water sources were about two miles away, so that chore was extremely important to her family.

After introductions, Memusi's brother, mother, and stepfather invited us into their hut. It was a small round structure made of sticks daubed with mud or plaster and topped with a thatched roof. We were tightly packed together. I noticed a simple cross hanging on the wall.

We were each served a brown chicken egg and hot coffee in a tin cup. We sat on short four-legged stools like those used when milking a cow. The hand-sculpted seats were surprisingly comfortable.

One of Memusi's daily chores is to walk two miles for water, which the donkey will carry home in a large jug.

The coffee was strong, the hot tin cup burning my lips and fingers with each sip. I was concerned about the egg. I wondered if it was cooked or raw. I decided I would eat it either way because I didn't want to offend the family. I watched Julius open his egg. It was boiled. What a relief!

While in the hut, we discussed Memusi's future. She didn't pass her grade-level exams at school, so she could not continue to high school. She had missed many school days because her mother had been ill, and Memusi was needed at home to care for the family and haul water.

What would she do now? What kind of future would she have with a 7th-grade education? She was just 13 years old.

Julius said Memusi had told him before my visit that she

wanted to attend a trade school and learn to be a tailor. I knew that women in some tribal countries are considered property, so I asked him if her parents would even allow Memusi to decide about her future. Julius said there was a possibility that since she couldn't continue her education, the family may have promised her as a wife to an older, wealthier man.

World Vision's support for girls and their families indirectly depends on the practice of "bridal promise." An older man will often be promised another man's daughter for his wife in exchange for money. World Vision has been educating relentlessly on the ethics of this tradition.

Julius, through the interpreter, asked Memusi's parents and older brother, one at a time, three critical questions about her future:

"Has Memusi been promised to a man?"

"Will you allow her to go to trade school?"

"Will you allow Memusi to choose what she wants to do?"

Every family member replied, "No, she has not been promised," and "Yes, she can go to trade school if that is what she chooses."

I was elated! A young woman's future was opened to her in that hour inside the small, dark hut. Mary and I would provide Memusi with a bicycle for transportation to school because young girls walking alone are targets for assault. After she graduated from trade school, we would provide a sewing machine to start her business. World Vision would make all the arrangements.

During the discussion, I considered the cross hanging on the wall, wondering if Memusi's family understood the love of

Jesus. I wondered if they knew He was working in all of us at that moment. I smiled and silently prayed for this family—I prayed that they could feel God's love in our questions and trust our intentions.

Memusi's family's hut. Memusi (right) carries her younger brother.

After our discussion in the hut, we went outside to find not only Memusi, but several neighbors who had come over to watch. I gave the family gifts: food staples, clothing, candy, and toys for Memusi and her little brother, and a shawl and fabric for her mother. Memusi's older brother and stepfather were very pleased with the goat. Goats are needed for meat and milk; if money is needed, they can be sold for cash.

To my surprise, Memusi and her mother presented me with a gift they had made for Mary. It was a beautiful traditional Masai decorative collar made of tiny, colored beads. The whole gift-giving event was narrated and directed by Julius and our Masai translator/goat farmer; every word spoken in Masai was translated into Swahili and then to English.

I gave the family a small map of the United States with a dot where Spencer is located, and I gave Memusi a picture of Mary and me with all our grandkids. I assured Memusi and her family, "Even though we are 9,000 miles away, remember that there is a family in America who loves you and prays for you."

I showed Memusi on a map where we live. The lollipops were among the gifts I gave to Memusi, which she shared with the neighbors who came to watch.

It filled me with joy to see the family and their friends peering over each other's shoulders to look at our family picture, pointing, smiling, laughing, and sucking on the lollipops I had given Memusi and her little brother.

Before leaving, we paused for pictures. Memusi's mother edged in closer to me, and Memusi took my hand and briefly put her head on my shoulder.

We Are the Children: Meeting Memusi, Part 2

On the long trip back to Arusha, I was emotionally and physically exhausted but also exhilarated. Memusi would go to a trade school where she would learn to be a tailor. She would be allowed to make her own decisions about her future, and she wouldn't be sold to a stranger to be his wife.

I was humbled and amazed that I was able to be part of the life-changing events that opened so many new possibilities for this family's only daughter. God works in mysterious ways, and I was thankful I could witness His love in action.

Since my visit in 2012, Memusi turned 21 and so has aged out of the World Vision sponsorship program. At that time, she had completed her trade school coursework, received the sewing machine, and opened her own tailoring shop. She was also renting space to other young women, helping them to get their start as tailors. It is truly difficult to express how happy and proud we are of her.

On the last Sunday of the VIMM mission trip, I was asked to speak at a church service. After my experience with Memusi's family, I wanted to reassure this congregation that we are all the same and that the Church worldwide is fed and grows through unity of faith in the love of Christ everywhere.

An interpreter passed along every word I spoke, so I relied on smiles and handshakes to determine that they understood. I wanted so much not to say or do anything to cause these lovely people to feel inferior to Westerners. Regardless of our station in life or where we were born, we are the same.

In some ways, I left feeling inferior to them. These people are tested to the end of endurance each day, yet they seem so happy. Most Americans have so much, but so many can't seem to find contentment.

I will always remember how the children would run to us

laughing with joy, grabbing the hands of those strange pale people, fascinated by and touching the hair of the blonde nurses. They walked beside us, holding hands with us as if they were our own children.

I heard a missionary speaker at a conference say, "The most important thing a missionary must do when coming into a country is first to discover the work the Spirit that has already done."

I saw God working with Memusi and her family on our trip to Tanzania and in the church that gathered on our last Sunday. We began nothing new. We didn't make big changes for the people of Arusha. But we were blessed to tag along, lend a hand, and reinforce what God has already done and will continue to do.

34
My Grandma, She Wrote Me a Letter

Our first grandchild, Jack, was born in January 2000, followed closely by Timothy in April 2000. After that came Allison, Anna, Sam, Charlie, Benjamin, Trevor, and Rowan in rapid succession, and lastly, Caleb in 2008.

Yup, you counted correctly: Ten grandchildren in eight years. Family gatherings were noisy and chaotic, but they have provided many sweet memories for us as grandparents. As I write this, the grandkids range in age from 14 to 23. The oldest was married to Makayla this past summer, whom we count as our 11th grandchild.

Although I have given little pieces of advice here and there to each grandchild since they were old enough to communicate, I feel like I should provide additional "information" to them as a group that I may have missed over the years. (And because, at ages 45, 47, and 49, my own children probably don't need my advice anymore.)

To that end, I'm sharing this open letter to my grandchildren:

Dear Grandchildren,

The purpose of this letter is to share our wisdom as grandparents based on 70+ years of life experience. (You didn't ask for our advice, but that never stopped me before. Just ask your parents.) So here we go, in no particular order:

Mind your Ps and Qs: *When Grandpa Steve and I were young parents and Joe, Aaron, and Laura were little, we would tell our kids, "Remember your P's and Q's!" They heard that line often enough to know that "P" stood for patient, polite, and pleasant, and "Q" for quiet and calm.*

Our kids were good spellers, so they figured out fairly early that "calm" didn't start with a "q." But they knew what we meant when we went into a restaurant or a friend's home and firmly reminded them, "Watch your P's and Q's!" This rule still applies whether you are 14 or 23+, or in between, or 70+, for that matter. These are essential habits for you to learn as you progress through your lives.

Be kind. *What do I mean when I say, "Be kind?" Being kind includes a lot of behaviors you already know, so I'll just give you one very simple piece of advice you should practice daily: Take time to look people in the eyes and speak to them, even people you don't know. Some people make others feel invisible—don't be like those people. If talking to strangers makes you uncomfortable, at least smile at them. You never know what kind of day they're having, and a smile from another human being could make a big difference.*

Be generous. *Share your time, your money, and your talents. Volunteer, do community service projects already in place or come up with your own, give to worthy causes, lead praise and worship, and sing or play an instrument at nursing homes. The list is endless. But—and this is key—don't share your time, money, and talents only when your* *generosity is noticed by a crowd. Do it even when (especially when) no one is watching.*

If you see someone at a street corner with a sign made from a torn-up cardboard box that says they need cash for their next meal or to feed their family, give them a few bucks. While it's true that they may use it to buy alcohol or drugs, that's not for you to discern.

The Bible says: "If a man asks for your coat, give them your cloak as well." It doesn't say, "But be sure he or she will use it wisely." Maybe you'd feel better giving them a gift card to McDonald's or a gift certificate for a grocery store. That's okay, too. But don't look for excuses not to give.

Leave a place better than you found it. *Grandpa Steve has taken it upon himself to pick up items on the floor of a store or hang up clothing thrown over a rack. It's not his job as a customer, but he does it anyway. (I'm trying to follow his example, but some shoppers are so careless and just plain messy!)*

Grandpa also picks up garbage and pop bottles on the street, in a parking lot, on a beach, or in other public places and puts them in a receptacle. He doesn't do it just when other people are watching, but if they do see him, maybe they'll follow his example and start trying to leave places better than they found them, too. And then other people will see them and... Well, you get my drift.

Make the world a better place *by recognizing prejudice (because of race, age, religion, ability, citizenship, or whatever), criticism, and judgment when you see it. Speak out, and defend those who are being marginalized, oppressed, or exploited. Use your natural gifts and skills to improve the lives of others. Speak up when a person or group of people are being mistreated. You can start where you are right now: at school, athletic or music practice, your job, or church.*

Whatever you decide to do in life, do it well. *Always give it your best effort. That applies to a hobby or sport, going to college,* working at your job—everything you attempt. Don't look for the easy way out or try to just get by. Ultimately it never works. You are all bright, talented, and skilled young people. Your gifts are God-given. Don't squander them.

Try new things. *Visit new places, meet new people, and plan new experiences (preferably nothing dangerous, like motorcycle skydiving or alligator wrestling). Learn new things. Study subjects outside of your major. Do it just for the enjoyment of learning.*

I was shy and reserved when I was growing up. So, when I had the chance to go to Brazil as an exchange student while a junior in high school, I was very reluctant to sign on the dotted line. But Grandma Betty strongly encouraged me not to turn down this once-in-a-lifetime opportunity. I am so glad I took her advice. My Brazilian family and I have remained friends for the past 55 years. Grandpa and I and Grandma Betty visited them 20 years after my semester in Rio de Janeiro and again in 2022 in Canada, where they were visiting their children.

And speaking of friends: You will meet people you immediately feel close to, and they could be your friends for life. You will also meet people you care about, but they don't feel the same about you. That's okay. There's no point in forcing a friendship or changing who you are for them. But even if they don't choose to be friendly, treat them with respect anyway.

Choose the right life partner. *He or she may not be the first person you fell in love with. Grandpa wasn't my first love, and I wasn't his. We were both dumped, and we were crushed for a while. But God showed us that He had another, more perfect, plan for us.*

Honor your father and mother. *Always show respect for your mom and dad, even when they're wrong (and they will be wrong sometimes). Let them know you love them with your words, acts, and behaviors. Now that I think about it, there's probably nothing I've written that your parents haven't already taught you. But it bears repeating, and I hope these words remind you of how blessed you are to*

My Grandma, She Wrote Me a Letter

have excellent (but maybe not perfect) parents, so I'll continue...

You will make good choices, and occasionally, you will make bad choices. When you do, **learn from your mistakes.** *Grandpa and I didn't always make good choices. But somehow, our bad choices worked out okay; more importantly, we learned from them. (Case in point: Ask Grandpa about the stuffed pink pig he "won" for me at the Clay County Fair.)*

Grandpa and I love each other very much. There were times when we disagreed and times when we were angry with one another. And although our marriage hasn't been perfect, one thing has remained constant: we are committed to loving each other through whatever comes our way.

Please know that we love each of you unconditionally, too, as do your parents. You won't fully understand the love a parent has for a child until you have children and grandchildren of your own.

If you remember only one thought from this letter, remember this:

There is nothing you can do to make us love you more, and there's nothing you can do to make us love you less. Nothing!

All our grandkids on the beach the night before Jack and Makayla's wedding.

35
I'll Have to Say I Love You in a Song

I don't remember my parents ever talking about sex or even romance when I was growing up. I only knew about reproduction because I grew up around farm animals.

Maybe Mom and Dad thought that was all the education we needed regarding procreation. They might have been concerned that discussing sex on a human level may have been interpreted as an encouragement to experience it, and we were a conservative, religious family.

The relationship between parents and children in the Steele home was authoritarian, judgmental, and full of consequences. Dad and Mom were loving parents but heavy-handed regarding God's judgment, wrath, and hell. Those topics weren't open for debate or even discussion.

Our family's social life totally revolved around church and

church families. I relied on my high school classmates and the popular music of the 1960s instead of my parents to learn about boy/girl relationships. Being more social and developing communication skills, mixed with an interest in girls, was passed on to me exclusively by my friends. I watched and listened closely to their conversations with the opposite sex.

Music also filled a void in my life. In the evenings, I would go to the car and listen to the radio. Mom and Dad didn't appreciate popular music, so, alone in the car, I could listen to the music I liked. I was transported to a different world through the songs played on radio stations WLS Chicago and KOMA, Oklahoma City, but only if the weather was favorable for reception.

Even now, when I hear the oldies played, I am reminded of my high school days, and I see the faces and voices of my friends. I feel the friendship of classmates, and I remember that small part of my world where I had control.

When I was growing up in the little town of Sutherland in Northwest Iowa, there was an ice cream shop called Otie's. I loved that place not only for the ice cream but because going there was an adventure. It was a cool place to be on a hot summer day, literally and figuratively.

Otie's served ice cream, of course, but also ice-cold root beer and all the candy you could ever wish for. Top-access freezers held tubs of ice cream and ice cream bars made by Otie himself. Glass root beer mugs were also stored in the freezer so they'd be frosty when served. The back of the counter against the wall was lined with stainless steel malt and shake blenders.

There was a jukebox just inside the door of Otie's. It was a mysterious contraption. You could watch the machine arm pick up a single 45-rpm record, bring it back to the turn table, place it perfectly on the turntable, and the music would start. The older kids had money to spend on music. I didn't. But I got to listen to their music for free and watch them interact. They even danced sometimes.

*Many a tear has to fall, but it's all in the game...*was the opening phrase in the Tommy Edwards 1958 hit. The song could be heard outside Otie's on hot summer Saturday nights when the door was left open. It's the song that turned me into an instant romantic at the age of eight, along with others like it: "Put Your Head on My Shoulder," sung by Paul Anka, "I Only Have Eyes for You," by The Flamingos, and "Donna" by Richie Valens.

The stores stayed open late two nights a week in Sutherland. On Saturday nights, kids with cars cruised slowly up and down the four blocks of Main Street. One of the guys had a Ford Sunliner with a roof that could retract and fold into the trunk. Another had a brand new dark green Pontiac Catalina. Some cars were works-in-progress. One was an early '50s Mercury fastback coup that never saw completion. It was always covered in primer paint, and the guy who owned it probably liked it that way.

The guys with cars would park in front of Otie's Ice Cream Shop or the bowling alley with their doors and windows open, listening to music on the radio. By the '60s, "A Summer Place" was a No.1 hit. My brothers loved it as much as I did. It's odd that an instrumental song by Percy Faith and orchestra would be so popular in the age of rock and roll.

I first experienced being turned down by a girl at one of many church-sponsored roller-skating parties. A giggled "No" to an invitation to skate with this short, chubby, red-haired fourth grader leaves an emotional scar. "Cathy's Clown" by the Everly Brothers was a song that I loved.

I'll Have to Say I Love You in a Song

Besides being able to relate to the lyrics, their harmony was easy to sing along with. Plus, it was comforting to know someone else felt rejected. It made me feel more normal.

The skating rink category of songs was weighted with songs of angst: "I'm Sorry," "Devil or Angel," "Tell Laura I Love Her," and "Teen Angel" were wrought with emotion. Conversely, even a 10-year-old boy cheers up when skating to "Itsy, Bitsy, Teeny Weenie, Yellow Polka Dot Bikini."

Wednesdays were also open nights, and the Sutherland High School band would perform summer concerts in the park. Cars pulled up along the park's perimeter, and residents from town walked to the concerts.

Broadway musicals in the '60s were popular, some of which included songs that were hits on the radio. Our band played songs from *Westside Story* ("Maria"), *Man of La Mancha* ("The Quest"), and the theme from *The Sound of Music*. The band was excellent; spectators clapped or honked their car horns after every number. The concerts were popular with young and old residents and brought the community together.

Two artists spurred my interest in vocal music as I left junior high and began high school. Johnny Mathis had a hit with his rendition of "Maria" from *Westside Story*, and Andy Williams sang "Moon River" from the movie *Breakfast at Tiffany's*. Both singers had voices and vocal styles I tried to imitate. The romantic mood of these songs rubbed off on me as I entered high school. I really hoped to be some girl's special guy someday.

I could always relate to songs about the guy or girl from the wrong side of town falling in love, being spurned, and the ensuing pain. The Four Seasons' "Rag Doll" nearly tore my heart out. "Hurt So Bad," "Poor Side of Town," "Tracks of My Tears," and "Down in The Boondocks" evoked similar emotions. (Maybe I missed my calling as a romance novelist.)

"Cupid" and "I Love You More Today Than Yesterday" resonated with me in high school. They still trigger memories of a girl with whom I was comfortable having a conversation. She seemed to understand and accept my social ineptness. Over the noon hour, popular songs were played in the high school gym, and talking with her while listening to the music made me feel important and mature while we halfheartedly shot baskets. She and I went out on a few dates. Any girl who paid attention to me was labeled "My Girl" in my imagination.

The songs of the '60s stayed with me through high school and on into college. When I finally met Mary and then her mom, Betty, the song "Mrs. Brown You've Got a Lovely Daughter" by Herman's Hermits ran through my mind.

During the summer of 1970, after our first year of college, Mary suggested we spend the summer without commitments. She would be working in Wisconsin at a church camp, and I had a job lined up at a TV station and a small church in Iowa. The distance between us meant we probably wouldn't see each other for three months. "Save Your Heart for Me" and "See You in September" filled me with a combination of love, longing, and loneliness.

I wrote Mary some embarrassingly mushy letters that summer. I blame my lovesickness on The Righteous Brothers' songs "Unchained Melody" and "You're My Soul and My Heart's Inspiration." I reread one of those letters recently and was appalled at how sappy it was. I can only imagine how Mary felt when she read it, especially since she was the one who suggested we "take a break."

I have a theory that music and memories are stored together in the same parts of our brains. One supports the other, and it is essential to our memories to keep those songs alive.

One last musical memory: On a fall evening with a full moon, I was walking on a gravel road with a beautiful woman. I began singing to her from Engelbert Humperdinck's hit song:

If I could catch a star before it touched the ground, I'd place it in a box, tie ribbons all around, and I would offer it to you, a token of my love and deep devotion...

Why not simply say, "I love you," you ask?

That would come later.

Many letters were mailed between Mary and me during the summer of 1970. Judging from the size of the two stacks, I'd say she wrote as many to me as I wrote to her, even though she was the one who suggested we "take a break" for the summer.

36
This One's for You, Mom

My mom's 96th birthday would have been Friday, Feb. 17, 2022. Since her birthday was three days after Valentine's Day, it was like having two holidays in one week for our family.

My sister Susan, my brother Michael, and I always made a cake to surprise Mom when she came home from work on her birthday. We'd pool our resources to buy a present from Hazel's, a gift shop in Readstown, WI, where we grew up. Mom was always pleased with our meager efforts, especially after putting in a long shift as a nurse.

If you've read *Betty: A Memoir*, you know my mom's story. But there's another story I'd like to share. It's the story-after-the-story of *Betty: A Memoir*.

So much has happened since the book was published. I've met relatives I didn't know existed, and I've visited places that have special meaning for me now because of the book. And I've discovered a part of my family history that I hadn't

This One's for You, Mom

known about before.

Some of the stories are incredible, many are sentimental, a few are embarrassing, and some are humorous. I want to share one of my favorites that could be filed in all four categories.

But first, let me bring you up to speed in case you haven't read *Betty*. Or maybe you have read it, but it's been a while, and you may have forgotten the details. Here's a quick summary:

My parents separated due to my dad's problem with alcohol when I was 4, Susan was 5, and Mike was 3. Mom loaded her three children onto a Greyhound bus and moved us from Florida back to her parent's home in Readstown. Despite being the only kid in grade school without a father, I had a mostly happy childhood.

My mom was a respected and well-liked nurse, working full-time to support her family. When her children were grown, she took a nursing position in Saudi Arabia, which enabled her to travel to 29 countries on five continents during her time off from the hospital.

After retiring, Mom moved to Iowa to be near her two daughters and her grandchildren. She was an active, healthy retiree, enjoying life with family and friends when she was diagnosed with terminal cancer. Susan and I cared for her at home until her death 32 days later.

Months later, I realized I was not dealing well with Mom's death. I struggled with grief, and along with the grief came anxiety. I started writing letters to my mom, sharing memories from the early days in Readstown and through the time we spent together after her diagnosis. Writing proved to be therapy for me—it helped me heal. The letters became part of the book I didn't know I was writing.

One day not long after *Betty: A Memoir* was published, I received a letter postmarked Viroqua, WI. I was puzzled because I didn't recognize the return address or name of the sender—Barb Nelson. Even though I grew up a few miles from Viroqua, and my mom worked at the Viroqua Hospital, I hadn't lived in the area for 52 years.

I opened the letter and was stunned and delighted to find it was from my childhood babysitter. She said she had always wondered what happened to our family. Then she picked up a copy of *Betty* and read it.

I didn't remember her because I was three years old at the time, but she remembered me, my siblings, and especially my mom. She shared her memories, including one that read: "Susan was tall and thin, and you were chubby with reddish blonde hair." Yup. Those descriptions were accurate.

Barb didn't have a computer, but we continued to communicate by letter and phone. We set a meeting date for when I'd be in Viroqua for a book signing. I was looking forward to meeting her, and she sounded excited about getting together, too.

However, when Steve and I arrived in Viroqua, I called Barb several times to touch base before the event, but I kept getting her answering machine. We drove to Barb's trailer court, but I didn't have her address. So, I googled her name, hoping to find her street address and house number.

I was crushed when the first entry that popped up for "Barb Nelson" was her obituary. Barb Nelson, age 88, of Viroqua, had died shortly before my book event. I was sad and disappointed that I'd missed my chance to meet her by just a few days.

This One's for You, Mom

The obit said a memorial service would be the next day with the family present to greet mourners. It would be at noon—after my book signing in the morning and before another book event in the afternoon. We decided to attend, introduce ourselves to the family, leave a copy of *Betty,* and express our sympathy for the loss of this woman who was obviously very fond of my mother and cared for my brother, sister, and me.

When we arrived at the church, we met several of Barb's family members, including her only daughter Linda. I explained that Barb and I had exchanged letters and phone calls after she had read *Betty*. I didn't want to take up too much of the family's time as there was getting to be a crowd of mourners, but Linda was interested in talking to me about the book. She said she'd thought about writing a memoir and had many questions about the process. We exchanged email addresses and promised to continue our conversation electronically.

Steve and I slipped away just before the service began, glad we'd made the effort. Everything had worked together perfectly. It was like it was meant to be.

Several weeks later, I was stunned to find another letter in our mailbox from Barb Nelson. I immediately thought this was some kind of scam—someone pretending to be Barb Nelson who saw her obituary and was using her name in a fraudulent manner.

But that didn't quite add up. Slowly, the realization crept into my mind that the woman, Barb Nelson, whose service we had attended, was not my babysitter, Barb Nelson.

What are the chances that there are **two** Barb Nelsons in the town of Viroqua (population 4,504) who were both 88 years old?

In the letter, my babysitter Barb apologized for not returning my calls and not coming to the book signing. There had been a family emergency that weekend that took her away. She hoped we could meet another time.

Still having a tiny bit of doubt, I called Barb's phone number and heard her familiar voice say hello.

How do you start a conversation like that?

"Hi, Barb. Is it really you?" Or maybe more direct but casual: "Barb, did you happen to pass away recently?"

As I began to tell Barb the story, she interrupted me before I could get all the words out, saying, "You went to the wrong Barb Nelson's funeral, didn't you?"

We both burst into laughter. I know... totally inappropriate. Barb went on to say there are (were) **three** Barb Nelsons, all about the same age, living in Viroqua.

After initially experiencing the joy of knowing that Barb, my babysitter, hadn't died, the horror followed when I realized I'd have to explain my faux pas to Linda, the other Barb Nelson's daughter. I knew I had to call her (she had been so kind and patient with me at the funeral), but I was tempted to email her.

I tried to keep my composure as I told her what had happened—that this perfect stranger crashed her mother's funeral and used up a big chunk of her time, taking her away from real mourners—and then tried to convince her that it wasn't a scam.

Her reaction? There was a long pause as I grew more anxious, and then she giggled! We talked for a half hour. Before hanging up, Linda said she appreciated my call and hoped we could continue our email correspondence. I was so relieved!

I wish I could share this story with Mom; she would love it! But I think she knows. Call me crazy, but I feel her presence every day. And, 12 years after her death, I think of her every time I see the number 444. As she lay dying, she told us, "Just remember: 444." We see 444 often—on a clock, a license plate, a billboard, our odometer. It may sound silly, but when I see those numbers, I feel like she's thinking of us.

On Friday, Feb. 17th, Susan and I will celebrate our mom's birthday together with lunch and a birthday cake while enjoying a view of the Gulf—one of Mom's favorite places. And she will be there with us.

Happy Birthday, Mom! We miss you, and we love you!

Happy Birthday, Mom!

37
I Am a Rock, I Am an Island

I grew up an Iowa farm boy in what, at first glance, appeared to be a typical, perhaps even ideal, 1950s family. But from my perspective, as the youngest of six children, we were far from perfect.

I wanted our family to be happy, serene, and fun. We weren't. My dad seldom displayed those qualities. Though he had softer moments with the family occasionally, I felt like I had to walk on eggs around him most of the time. I still wonder, at 71, if I served any purpose—if I mattered—to Dad or the rest of the family. I was four years younger than my next oldest sibling. A cute but unnecessary latecomer.

Our small farm provided for a family of eight, so my dad's life focused on farm work. We took just one short vacation away from the farm to the Black Hills of South Dakota. It was meant as a sendoff for my oldest sister, Virginia, who would soon leave for college.

My two sisters were 12 and 10 years older than me, and my memories of them are distant and fuzzy. My mom says they loved showing me off to their friends when I was an adorable baby, so they get bonus points for that from me.

Phil was easygoing and tenderhearted. Tim and Tom were both quick to anger. That resulted in fierce, almost daily confrontations. Those two boys would fight like cats and dogs. A touch football game in the front yard would frequently end up with a full tackle, and sometimes fists would fly. I would cry, yell, and beg for them to stop. I hated the fighting.

Family tension often centered around Dad, the older boys, and the quality of work or completion of a job. A whiny response or outright defiance of Dad was sure to raise his ire. In an age of "children should be seen and not heard," either response was asking for trouble.

Phil bore the brunt of Dad's demands. Being the oldest son carried with it high expectations. I was young enough that I usually wasn't expected to work outside with the other boys, for which I was grateful. I didn't like the anxious feeling I got when Dad was impatient or angry, and I tried to avoid conflict whenever possible.

When squabbling erupted amongst us kids, my parents were quick to say, "You just mind your own business." I took their advice, and I learned to enjoy being alone.

Gradually, my siblings moved away from home, and I was given more responsibilities. I was a high school freshman when Tom was a senior, and when he went off to college, an unexpected vacuum opened in my life.

Tom and I hadn't been especially close growing up, but our family dynamic changed suddenly. Our family of eight was now a family of three. When Dad had designated farm chores, Tom was the first to be recruited, and I was next in line. With him gone, there was no longer a buffer between my dad and me.

I loved my parents and wanted to please them. I had a compliant personality, worked hard, and did as I was told. But I also yearned for the freedom I'd had in my younger years when I could disappear without my absence being noticed.

My social life revolved around church activities, school events, music, and sports. I used every opportunity to get involved in activities that would get me out of the house. I went on my first date during my sophomore year. I would stretch out those dates to last as long as possible, using half-truths, exaggerations, and outright lies to explain missing a curfew.

However, I wasn't a good liar, and my last three years at home caused considerable concern for my mom. I'm not sure how much, if any, my dad worried. Instead, I think he carefully planned how he'd respond to my first acts of rebellion and nip them in the bud.

After coming home extremely late from a date one night, Dad woke me up at 5 a.m. the next day to do the chores, dig postholes, and fix fences all day. I worked hard and didn't complain—the work builds muscle. Even though I was sensitive to my parents' disapproval, I would risk it to spend time away from home with friends.

Mom was so worried about me that she asked my sister, Sue, for advice about my behavior. Sue was married and a young mother at the time who was known for speaking her mind when the situation called for it. She read me the Riot Act for coming home late and for dating girls from another church denomination (which was one of Mom's primary concerns).

Sue said my actions showed disrespect for my parents and for our family. I realized her lecturing me was motivated by love and concern. She showed me who I was and that what I did mattered to the family and to God.

I hadn't realized how much I depended on my siblings as examples and guideposts. I began to understand the difference they'd made in my life. As a boy, they made the decisions, and I followed their example. I didn't have to make many decisions for myself.

In the summer before my junior year, my foster brother Keith came into our home and into my life. Keith was a year younger than me. We both played football and participated in other school activities, so we drove to school together in our old farmwork car.

In all honesty, I was a little irked. It seemed to me I had been given the responsibility of making sure this relative stranger behaved himself and was safe in our care. I had my own questionable choices to be responsible for, and I didn't like the idea of Keith being involved in or knowing my not-so-sterling behaviors.

Ironically, having Keith nearby and watching my every move became a good thing. I started thinking more deeply about how I felt when I began losing the mentors in my life as my siblings left home.

I was pursued by the idea that it was time to demonstrate responsibility, and I began to change. Most people would call it simply "growing up." Keith and I developed a close and mutually supportive relationship.

I have often thought of my family as "distant but close." The lyrics of a song by Simon and Garfunkel described my family, and me in particular, during those early years: "I am a rock, I am an island..."

Then I began losing members of my family. There are only three of us left. Now there is empty space, occupied only by silence and memories. I began to understand how much my parents, brothers, and sisters affected my life with their mere presence and example.

Dad died following a series of health issues, and Tim died just 17 days later in early 2002.

Sue passed away after a courageously fought 15-year battle with brain cancer in 2014. I will always remember her for caring enough to make me stop and think about my actions and to tell me that I mattered.

My strict but loving and kindhearted mother died at 96, five days before my 65th birthday in 2016. I felt like an orphan. I had retired seven years earlier, in part so that I could spend more time with her. During those visits, we strengthened our relationship through our conversations. She helped me understand more clearly the power of faith and what it means to truly believe and trust in God. Her faith in Jesus defined who she was.

The firstborn of our family, Virginia, and family settled in Tennessee. In 1973, Mary and I, with our new baby, Joey, moved to Tennessee after I decided to earn a teaching degree at Milligan College.

Virginia and her husband Richard invited our family of three to live with them until we found housing. I will always be indebted to them for that voluntary intrusion into their lives. Her husband has passed away, and Virginia now lives comfortably in assisted living near her two sons and their families. She has advanced dementia and no memory of them or me. (Since this chapter was written, Virginia passed away peacefully in her sleep in July 2023.)

I regret not knowing these three remarkable women better, but I appreciate their powerful influence on my life. My brothers were excellent examples to me as well.

Phil had a patient and kind heart that allowed him to play second fiddle to his sisters. His modest and humble manner won him the friendship and admiration of many of his classmates.

Tim and I became close while we attended Milligan College at the same time, taking education classes, earning degrees together, and graduating in the winter of 1974. I appreciated his support. Like me, he was a teacher and coach.

Tom shepherded me during my freshman year at Nebraska Christian College. He made me feel valued. He also let me borrow his car to take Mary out on our first date!

Dad showed me that anything could be fixed when he patiently repaired my broken bicycle. (That is the first time I have used "patient" and "dad" in the same sentence.) Thanks, Dad.

To my imperfectly perfect family: I love you all.

The Steele family at Doris and Silas's anniversary celebration: (Back) Phil, Keith Logan, Tim, Tom, and Steve; (Front) Virginia, Doris, Silas, and Sue.

38
I've Had the Time of My Life

Today, I am 71 years, six months, and 24 days old. Put another way, I am closer to 72 than 71.

Seventy-two sounded really old to me a few decades ago, but it's beginning to seem much younger these days. I don't feel like I'll be 72 soon, but I have noticed some signs that I have aged.

Sometimes I catch a glimpse of my reflection in a window and see an old lady who is stooped over, and then I realize it's me. I hear my mom's voice in my head: "Stand up straight, Mary! Shoulders back!" She said that to me when I was a teenager and even after I became an adult. Now I understand why Mom thought slouching was a bad habit I needed to break—the sooner, the better—before it became permanent.

(A side note: I think the current condition of my spine

probably has more to do with my hunched look than not standing up straight, but I know Mom had my best interest in mind.)

Other signs? Let's talk about wrinkles. I'll admit it—wrinkles bother me. And my neck... When did my neck start looking like a turkey's wattle?

Years ago, the late Nora Ephron wrote a book titled, "I Feel Bad About My Neck." In it, she said the only part of the body that cosmetics, Botox, filler, collagen, and surgery couldn't improve was a saggy, wrinkly neck. I've heard that there is a surgical procedure now for neck sag. Like Nora, I, too, feel bad about my neck—but not bad enough to have surgery.

As of this writing, February 2022, I've had only two operations in my life. (There have been two more since, but I'm not going there now.) The first was a tonsillectomy when I was six, even though I don't think I ever had tonsillitis. My sister was having a tonsillectomy the same day. (There may have been a two-for-one special—my mom was frugal.)

To ease any concern I may have had about the procedure, Mom and the doctors told Susan and me that we could eat as much ice cream as we wanted after surgery, so I looked forward to it. She didn't tell me that after your tonsils are yanked out, you are too sick and your throat too sore to eat anything, including ice cream. (I've had trust issues with authority figures ever since.)

My second operation was 62 years later. I had Chiari surgery which involved a neurosurgeon removing a piece of my skull to relieve pressure on my brain. A painful year-long recovery followed the surgery. I'm fine now, but I'd rather look like a wrinkled, wattled, and stooped 100-year-old than undergo any type of surgery again.

I've Had the Time of My Life

I find it especially concerning that my memory is fading. I sometimes forget if I've brushed my teeth just minutes after I've done so, and I have to touch the bristles to see if they're wet. Same with applying deodorant.

> **One minute you're young and fun, and the next you're turning down the stereo in your car to see better.**

Similarly, I can't remember if I've taken my pills. I finally switched to using one of those day-by-day pill boxes to double-check to make sure I took them on the right day. (Now, if only I could remember what day today is.)

What's really embarrassing is when my memory loss is apparent to family and friends. I'm sure I've told them the same story countless times, but I can't remember with whom I've already shared it. Or how many times.

Remembering dates is also a problem for me. Recently, someone asked me when our daughter was born, and after stammering around, I told her, "1877." I was off by a century. I meant 1977, of course. I have no idea where 1877 came from. I'm sure she thinks I'm losing it.

On the other hand, I've never had a good memory. When I was a kid, there was a time (okay, several times) when I rode my bike to Glass General Store to pick up a loaf of bread or other items for my mom and then walked home, forgetting my bike propped up against the store. Later in the day, I was puzzled when I couldn't find my bike.

Mom used to say almost daily, "Mary, you'd lose your head if it weren't screwed on!" Not a real confidence builder for a pre-teen.

So, maybe my memory hasn't changed all that much over the past seven decades. As I consider the possibility, I think maybe I should have named this episode "Still Hazy After All These Years."

And then there's technology. Nothing has caused me as much frustration as learning to use electronic devices, including my laptop and cell phone.

Here's an example:

I cannot, for the life of me, remember how to take a screenshot on my laptop, even though I've done it several times. I always have to google the instructions, and I realize that there is a *Print Screen* button on my keyboard. (Just ask my daughter, who has to field my frantic calls and texts, crying out for help.)

This morning, I accidentally took a selfie while reading an email from a high school classmate, and my picture popped up in my reply. That wouldn't have been so bad, except I had just gotten up and looked like a creature from the Black Lagoon. Unfortunately, the photo didn't go just to the sender but to all 16 or so classmates who, like us, are wintering in Orange Beach, AL.

I knew I could delete the post and photo, but in my panic, I couldn't remember how. After about five minutes of frantically pressing every key and combination of keys, the selfie finally disappeared. But probably not before it had terrified several friends who happened to click on my reply before I managed to delete the mug shot.

I could go on, but I think that's enough of the downside to getting older. There are some advantages, too. Here's a list I found online:

- In a hostage situation, you are likely to be released first.
- There's nothing left to learn the hard way.
- Things you buy now won't wear out.
- You host a party, and the neighbors don't complain about the noise—in fact, they don't even realize you're having a party.
- Your investment in health insurance is finally beginning to pay off.
- Your secrets are safe with your friends because they can't remember them either.
- Your supply of brain cells is down to a manageable size.

But, seriously, folks, there are benefits to growing older. Here are a few that I've observed or experienced:

1. **Financial security**. Raising three kids on a teacher's salary was, well, let's just say, challenging. Before his first teaching job, we were making just enough to scrape by. Even after Steve started teaching, he worked most summers to supplement his income.
2. **Independence**. Since we retired, we pretty much do what we want when we want. Some people would call that self-indulgence, and they'd probably be right. We've done little to earn an almost carefree retirement, and we don't take the credit for it. Neither do we take it for granted.

3. **Good health.** A retired friend shared a description of getting older that is probably pretty accurate: There's the Go-Go '60s, the Slow-Go '70s, and No-Go '80s. I'd say we're still in the "Go-Go" phase, but we're keenly aware that could all change with a single unexpected life-changing diagnosis or accident.
4. **Kids are grown.** At our age, we no longer worry about our kids. They've proven they can make it on their own without our supervision, advice or financial aid. (Although we still give them advice occasionally. Free of charge.)

And the biggest bonus of getting older?

5. **Grandchildren!** We have been blessed with ten responsible, bright, and tender-hearted grandkids who, along with their parents, are the lights of our lives.

Even when I am way past my golden years, I'll continue to look forward to my birthdays because getting older is something to celebrate. Many of our friends and family members didn't have that privilege.

If I haven't convinced you that there are advantages to getting older, consider this bit of wisdom from Kitty O'Neil Collins:

"Aging appears to be the only way to live a long life."

39
I'm Still Standing

Wherever adolescent males are gathered, there will likely be dumb and dangerous ideas in the midst of them. My brothers and our friends were accomplished at advancing stupid ideas into risky stunts, and although I joined in the hijinks, I was too young to take responsibility for the outcomes.

Farming involves plenty of risks without boys inventing other activities that could result in maiming or death. According to the U.S. Bureau of Labor Statistics, farming is twice as deadly as police work and five times more so than being a firefighter.

However, the farm is the perfect location to try these stunts since the amount of space on the farm creates distance from the house. Parents don't always know what's happening "out there."

Questionable activities almost always begin with a curious thought explored by inquisitive young minds. Combine that with a lack of close supervision, and disastrous results can and do occur. It's fair to say I am lucky to be alive and in good health, with all my limbs intact, at age 70+.

Here's a random list of stupid stunts and experiments we boys accomplished "all by ourselves" and sometimes were prompted by watching TV.

Stupid Stunt #1: A group of boys gathered at the Steele house for lunch on a Sunday afternoon. One of the older friends asked my brother, Tim, "Do you think a 22 bullet would fire if we shot it with a BB gun?" There was laughter because a 22-cartridge is small and would be difficult to hit.

The challenge was met with enthusiasm, and all agreed we should try it. We set it up by putting the bullet on the top of a fence post with everyone standing behind the shot, 10 yards away, to ensure their safety.

The guys took turns firing so we'd know who hit the bullet if it went off. After many misses, a hit! The cartridge went off with a pop, and the bullet didn't hit anyone.

However, established science tells us that for every action, there is an opposite and equal reaction. The bullet casing flew backward and injured the shooter's hand, who was the same kid who had conceived the idea. Talk about scientific justice.

The injury makes sense from a scientific standpoint, but unfortunately, it doesn't make the wound any easier to explain to the parents.

Stupid Stunt #2: The same group of boys came up with this fun idea. We had a windmill tower on our farm and a large amount of old twine that had been tied around hay bales. The idea was to create a zipline by braiding a 120-foot rope from those five-foot pieces of twine. It took several days for us to braid and connect all those short sections tightly together.

Next, we rescued an old pulley from the barn and ran the rope through the pulley so it could roll along the rope. A burlap bag stuffed with straw was tied to the pulley to hold on to. Then, one end of the rope was tied to the windmill tower 20 feet above the ground and the other end to the bottom of a nearby tree. Voila! We had our own zipline.

This is like the windmill on the Steele farm; ours has since been taken down. Note that it offers many places to start a zipline.

It worked as is the nature of physical systems, and we enjoyed ziplining for a while. Then, when one of the older boys grabbed the bag tied to the pulley and began flying down, a section of the rope pulled apart. He plummeted, hitting the ground first with his feet and then with his head, from about 10 feet up.

The kid had no broken bones, only a bruised ego, and we had learned the literal meaning of the expression, "He went head over heels."

Stupid Stunt #3: I was always impressed by the television images of tanks at war that were equipped with flame throwers. How do flame throwers work? I decided to find out for myself.

Saturdays were my usual days to take out the trash and haul it to the burn pile where we disposed of flammable garbage. Since fire fascinated me, I looked forward to this chore.

I came up with an idea for making my own flame thrower. After I started the garbage burning, I filled one of my dad's oil cans with diesel fuel. It was the kind of oil can that had a lever you pushed to make it squirt a long stream of fuel.

Fortunately for me, diesel burns more slowly than gas. When I squirted it on the fire, there was a long string of flame along the fuel stream. I could even write my name in flames.

I never gave any thought to the extreme danger just inches from my hand. I can only imagine how different the outcome might have been had I chosen to use gasoline instead of diesel fuel. It could have been a life-or-death decision.

Stupid Stunt #4: Our windmill tower was right next to the road ditch, which was filled with snow in the winter. We boys would jump off the lowest tower section, about six feet high, into the deep snow. When that height lost its thrill, we moved up to the second section, about twelve feet up, and jumped from there.

We didn't notice that the snow was getting packed down from all the jumping, so we no longer had a nice cushion of snow to soften our landing. When I landed on my feet after jumping from the third section, about 18 feet in the air, it jarred my brain, and my head hurt from the impact. We decided not to make that jump from the third section again. Sometimes we learned from our experiences.

Stupid Stunt #5: Our family had a 410 single-shot shotgun we used for pheasant hunting. It's a small gun and not very powerful. My mom probably thought it was safe for us boys to hunt with and that there was little chance any kids—or pheasants—would be harmed.

Tom had the idea to change a shotgun cartridge from birdshot to a slug so he could hunt deer with the gun.

"Is that possible?" you might ask.

Well, yes, but you might also ask, "Is it a good idea?"

We pried open the cartridge at the crimped end, dismantled the wadding, and saved the lead BBs. Since lead has a low melting temperature, we liquified it in the skillet Mom used to fry eggs on our kitchen stove.

We poured the melted lead into a homemade mold made from a piece of wood with a hole drilled in it. When it had hardened, we chipped the wood away to get the lead slug out, filed it smooth, and dropped it down the gun barrel 50 times. We assumed that if it went through smoothly, it would be safe to fire the gun.

We reassembled the cartridge, put it in the gun, and went out to the grove for a test shot. We stood out of harm's way behind Tom. For extra safety, Tom would turn his head on the chance the slug stuck in the barrel and the gun blew apart. I believe his thinking was that he would rather lose his hearing and keep his sight if things didn't go well.

Surprisingly, the test worked as planned. But we never tried it again. I thought there were too many potentially dangerous results. I think Tom felt lucky that the gun didn't blow up, and I'm not sure he really wanted to hunt deer anyway.

Stupid Stunt #6: My brothers and cousins all liked to read Hot Rod magazines. They loved talking about cars and engines and how to make more horsepower so their cars would go faster.

My cousins had an old 1950 Chevy coupe with a six-cylinder on which they had put new and very loud glass-pack mufflers. Apparently, they thought more noise made a car go faster.

My brothers drove the family's old 1953 Kaiser 6-cylinder sedan. It was the first car my dad had ever bought brand new. The only modification we'd made was the locking pliers we used to replace the broken shifter handle.

One summer, the Chevy boys challenged the Kaiser boys to a race. These two machines dueled it out side-by-side on the county blacktop road into town. My oldest brother, Phil, was driving, and he had his foot on the floor. Both cars were straining with every ounce of power they had.

My heart was pumping away in excitement and anxiety during the race. What if a car came at us over the crest of those hills? What if a tire exploded at 100 mph?

The Chevy never made headway against the Old K, both traveling 100 mph. To me, the Kaiser was just our old car. I never imagined it could go that fast. All this happened on worn-out tires with the cords showing where there should have been tread.

We are lucky Dad didn't find out about the Kaiser vs. Chevy duel. It was a dangerous race using ill-prepared equipment. However, I recall my dad telling some of his cronies that our '57 Dodge could do 120 mph. It felt good to know he was once a little like his sons.

The incident brought back memories of lyrics from a popular song of the time:

"Son, you're gonna drive me to drinkin' if you don't quit driving that hot-rod Lincoln."

Like most kids, we were curious and simply trying to discover how the world works. This observation by American author Carolyn Haywood sums up why I write and share these memories:

"Children are not only innocent and curious but also optimistic and joyful and essentially happy. They are, in short, everything adults wish they could be."

This Kaiser is the first new car that Silas purchased. The family dog, Bullet, is in the foreground.

40
These Are a Few of My Favorite Things

I was recently asked the question: What are your favorite possessions?

My immediate response: That depends.

Does the question mean intangible things like your health, marriage, and faith? What about living things like family, friends, and pets?

Or, does it mean: "If your house was on fire and you had just enough time to gather your favorite things, what three things would you take?"

I interpreted "favorite things" to mean tangible items you can see and touch, but not living things.

Since I'm seldom at a loss for words or shy about sharing my opinions, I'll answer the question as I interpret it; but before I do, I want to share how some of my friends and family members responded when I asked them the same question. Here are their responses, slightly edited and in no particular order:

Lori: All of my original Julie Vandeberg art, but especially "She Dressed in Yellow," my dad's gold watch, and the quilt my sister made me using real Japanese fabrics.

Carson: Kindle, my bed, and my phone.

Sheila: Passport, Tempurpedic pillow, and my ceiling fan.

Nicole: My jewelry box. Inside the box, I have irreplaceable (not necessarily super valuable) pieces from our grandmothers, my parents and husband, and a couple of little notes from my kids; my photo hard drive (photos, videos, and so many memories! And super hard to replace); keepsake box filled with notes, letters, my kid's handprints, old photos, etc.; our piano, a gift from my parents, the maker is no longer making pianos, and I love that the brand is my maiden name.

Joe: A car, my wife's jewelry box, and laptops.

Trevor: My brother's barnwood entertainment center filled with a gaming system and projector, his bed, and the piano.

Millie: Photos/keepsakes, garden/yard, a good novel. In case of fire, IDs, lockbox, phone.

Laura (Our daughter, a professional photographer): Our Shutterfly albums; my laptop with all my client photos and family photos; my autographed copy of *Betty: A Memoir*; maybe the framed map of the states with a pic from each state we've visited.

(Judging from the laughing emoji she put next to *Betty* and the fact that she added another third choice, I'm questioning her sincerity about including the book I wrote and autographed appearing on her favorite things list...)

Margo: My dishwasher, our condo in Arizona.

(Not sure how she'll manage that if the condo building is on fire, but like I told Margo, there are no wrong answers to this question.)

Linda: My wedding rings, family pictures, and the cross necklace Barry made me from my mother's everyday silverware because it holds memories of family and because Barry cares enough to make it for me. Fourth would be the stringer pin my dad used when he went squirrel hunting. It is worthless in value except to me and the memories I have of it. Fifth would be my Hopalong Cassidy mug I used all the time as a little kid. When it comes down to it, it's all stuff, but it is the sentimental endearment each holds.

Jane: Photos/scrapbooks/videos of kids when younger and of my parents; my rings, Christmas ornaments (because we have ornaments commemorating our lives—ones we got when we got married, on vacations, to commemorate our kids' births and interests at various points in their lives, ornaments kids made over the years, ornaments that hung on parents' Christmas trees; St. Thomas round stained-glass window (because it's beautiful; from the church that I, my parents, and grandparents were baptized and married in, and it's not replaceable, especially since the church has been torn down; Santas made by Rita, my sister-in-law, which are not higher up on the list because I know I could beg a few from sisters-in-law if I lost all mine.

(I think Jane will need to move fast and will also need a truck to remove all her favorite things in case of a fire.)

Anonymous: My wedding ring, a mug we bought on a

special vacation (I love the shape and the design on the mug as well as the people and places I am reminded of every time I drink from it), and our acreage.

I was surprised with the amount of interest generated by asking this question. Several respondents said they shared it with family members and had a lively discussion among the spouses and kids, who also listed their favorite things. Because of that, more people than I expected responded to the question, making this chapter the longest I've written yet.

Okay, so here are my answers:

What to take just before fleeing your burning home: This question is probably a no-brainer. I would grab essential papers like our will, title to our house and cars; baby, wedding, and other family photos that can't be replaced because some are 50+ years old; cash and credit cards; anything of great value such as jewelry, heirlooms, cash, etc.

Hopefully, our important papers and photos are all stored on a laptop or flash drive, so that would save a lot of time—and possibly our lives. Instead of rooting around looking for our miscellaneous documents (that may or may not be in our security box where they're supposed to be stored) as well as all those priceless photos, we would instead quickly pick up our two laptops and flash drives and get the heck out of there. (Keeping in mind that all those house insurance payments made over the past 50 years are finally paying off.)

So, back to the original question: ***What are your favorite possessions?*** I understand the question to mean those irreplaceable items that have significant sentimental or historical value, although they might not net me much cash on eBay.

My wedding ring would be at the top of my list. It's very

plain, made of white gold, engraved inside with the words, "We've Only Just Begun." That title of a song has proven to be true for us. At age 72, after being married for 52 years, we still feel like we've only just begun. (That may be because, at our age, we've forgotten most of the past five decades.)

Oh, by the way, did I mention that I asked Steve the burning house question, too? He emailed back to me his answers: *"Bike, baritone, and camper."* Note that he did **not** say wedding ring, wedding album, or marriage license.

I replied to his email with this: "I want a divorce!!!"

Actually, Steve's responses were honest and appropriate. Steve rides his bike almost every morning to stay in shape, even in the snow and on ice. He bought a battered-looking but sweet-sounding baritone and started playing almost five decades after graduating from high school. When he was out for band, he rented a horn, and so he'd never owned one of his own before. And although we both enjoy the camper, it's really his baby.

Enjoying a campfire with grandkids Caleb and Anna. Steve and I both agree that our little camper is one of our favorite things.

Steve's choices didn't actually surprise me. He gets his investment back on all of these things, and they provide him with activities he loves. (But not as much as he loves me, he claims. Maybe I'll rethink the divorce thing.)

Back to **my** list. Another item besides my wedding ring is a gold cartouche on a gold chain that spells "McSwain" in hieroglyphics. My mom, Betty McSwain, bought it on a trip to Egypt while working in Saudi Arabia as a nurse. She wore it every day. The same is true for me—I almost never take it off.

Another of my favorite things is a sapphire ring that our son, Joe, and daughter-in-law, Nicole, surprised me with a few years ago. I had given Nicole a sapphire ring that Mom bought when she worked in Saudi Arabia. The ring was made of some mystery metal, but all the sapphires were real. Nicole had a local jeweler craft three rings using the sapphires: one for herself, one for their daughter, Allison, and one for me. It is a reminder of the bond between three generations of women.

Nicole, Ally, and I have identical rings created from one of Betty's sapphire rings. My ring was a gift from Joe, Nicole, and family.

It's interesting that three of my favorite things are jewelry, especially since I've never considered myself a jewelry person. Occasionally I switch one of the rings with a different piece—usually something from Mom's extensive collection. Since most of her jewelry was purchased in the Middle East, the pieces my sister and I inherited are exotic designs. (Dare I say, *gaudy*?)

For example, Mom had rings and bracelets in the shape of gold cobras with ruby eyes. The cobra was a sign of royalty in early history. The pieces are safely tucked away in a safety deposit box at our bank, where they'll stay until my children and grandchildren inherit them.

I'm not sure if our house qualifies as a possession. (But like I told Margo, there are no wrong answers.) It's not new, large, or fancy, but it's light, bright, and simply decorated—some would say "sparsely decorated." If one word could sum up our home, I'd say it's peaceful. We like to travel, but no matter where we've been or how long we've been gone, I am always delighted to walk into our house after a trip.

My thanks to friends and family members who participated in this little poll and provided interesting, thoughtful, and varied responses for this chapter. Your lists and comments added significantly to this story.

By the way, I noticed no one included *"whiskers on kittens and warm woolen mittens..."*

My apologies to Julie Andrews.

41
Hit Me with Your Best Shot

I was forced to consider my mortality in 2014. I faced the possibility that I may not have tomorrow and began to realize the importance of how I live today. It was like God was talking directly to me.

After I retired from Spencer Community Schools, I taught an Introduction to Earth Science class at Iowa Lakes Community College. It was made up mostly of soccer athletes and non-traditional students.

I try to be interesting and enthusiastic when describing rocks, weather, space, oceans, and the environment to my students. One morning while lecturing, I may have been a little too passionate in my instruction.

We were nearing the end of the 90-minute session when I felt dizzy. I decided to end the session a few minutes early and dismiss the class. I sat down on a lab stool while talking to one of the students, and suddenly, the room and the people around me started to turn gray and dissolved into nothingness.

When I opened my eyes, I saw the faces of EMTs, students, and my wife, Mary. My first words were, "Well, that was a nice nap."

Truthfully, it was very pleasant until I tried to move my left arm. The pain was immense. I had fallen face-first on the floor with my nose and left cheek absorbing the blow, breaking my glasses and gouging an eye. My arm caught on the stool as I fell forward, causing my shoulder to be dislocated.

Word of my collapse spread quickly through the building. Mary worked at the college, and her office was just down the hall, so she was one of the first on the scene. It was decided that I should be taken to the hospital.

The experience was new for me. I was given the whole treatment you might see on a TV medical show—an ambulance racing to the hospital, lights flashing, EMTs scurrying around, pulse and blood pressure measurements taken, and a bag of fluid dripping into my arm.

Arriving at the ER, I learned a new term: *vasovagal syncope*. It sounded quite serious, but in layman's terms, it meant I had fainted. All that drama for a guy who passed out. I was embarrassed, though I have to say, I enjoyed the attention.

My ego was massaged a little when the doctor said I probably worked out too hard that morning (I had) without drinking enough water (also true), and I was dehydrated, along with being on my feet teaching for 1½ hours.

This would make a great story if I could say that during the

15 minutes I was out, I walked toward bright lights or saw angels. But I didn't remember anything while I was unconscious: not a thought, a sound, or an image. I wonder where my mind was in that 15-minute flash of nothing. It felt as though I was fast-forwarded like a television program to a completely different show when I awoke. I had a beating heart but no consciousness.

If you were to name any part of my body, I probably have injured it. My head, though, has taken the most abuse, starting as a youngster. I'm sure there are readers chuckling to themselves and thinking, "Well, that explains a lot about Steve."

When I was four years old, I fell asleep while visiting friends of our family in their home. My mom carried me to the door, and as she started down the steps toward the car, she tripped and fell with me in her arms. I landed on my head, and she landed on top of me. We drove directly to the hospital 20 miles away in Cherokee, where it took six stitches for the doctor to close the gash on my forehead.

I don't remember any part of the incident, but much later, Mom explained to me why I have a bump and a scar on my forehead. When I was older, I thoughtfully told her I was glad I had been there to cushion her fall.

Another accident occurred when I was 13 years old. Dad had sold a large load of straw to a neighbor whose farm was three miles east of ours. The exertion of loading the bales onto the wagon had left Tim, Tom, and me hot and sweaty. We looked forward to the cooling breeze we'd feel while sitting on the load of bales as the tractor pulled the wagon down the road.

I chose to ride on top of the bales, six layers high, with a few extra bales on top to sit on. I was about 15 feet in the air. Tom drove the tractor, and Tim rode the fender. It felt comfortably cool as we headed down the road toward our neighbor's farm.

I was very relaxed, enjoying the ride as we headed down a hill toward the Waterman Creek bridge. There was a deep ditch falling away from both sides of the road at either end of the bridge. Suddenly Tim began to wave frantically for me to jump.

The tractor hitch had broken loose and had come off the tractor. The wagon loaded with bales was out of control and was headed toward the deep ditch on the right side next to the bridge.

With so many things happening at once, I'm not sure if my memory of the accident is precise. I intended to jump down on the road but actually left the load headfirst. I think I must have tripped on the twine tied around a bale as I moved to the edge. That was the last thing I remember.

While I was unconscious, a farmer drove by, saw our situation, and took me back to our farm. Mom drove me from our house to the hospital. I became vaguely aware of being in our family car when we were almost to the ER.

I'm told that I landed on my face and head on the side of the gravel road. (I'm glad it wasn't concrete.) I must have tried to catch myself with my arms extended in front of me as both bones in my right forearm were broken. While being wheeled into the hospital, I remember thinking my arm looked as if it was pointed in the wrong direction. My face was scratched, but no stitches were needed.

High school sports also provided opportunities for accidents and injury. In the late winter of my sophomore year, track season workouts had already started for the track team. Winter was trying to become spring but was having a difficult time accomplishing that task. We tried to practice outside whenever there was a reasonable amount of spring warmth.

I didn't have the gift of speed my father possessed when he was in high school. I had grown into a chunky, solidly built lad, more square than tall or fast.

Competing in the shot put event for Sutherland High School in 1969.

As a specialist in the field events of shot put and discus, I was in the business of lifting weights and developing muscle explosiveness to push, or "put," the 12-pound iron ball and throw the discus as far as possible. A close friend, Dan, and I were both aspiring shot and discus throwers whose prowess in those events would later earn us the title of the "Dynamic Duo" (a reference to Batman and Robin) from team members.

As throwers in the field events, we did everything together. We ran workouts, lifted weights, and practiced throwing drills and techniques. We would challenge and compete against one another in practice to push each other toward constant improvement.

On this day, Dan was having a bad practice and was upset with himself after a poor throw. I gave him some helpful advice about technique and rolled the 12 lb. iron ball back to him.

In his frustration, Dan immediately grabbed the shot, went back into the circle, and put the shot again. At that exact moment, I was bent over, marking his previous effort with a stick, when his "put" descended and struck my head with a glancing blow.

I don't remember feeling the impact or experiencing pain. I had no thoughts, no images in my mind. I was unconscious. I was told later that Dan ran across the practice field to get our coaches. They put a towel on my head to control bleeding and applied ice to minimize swelling.

I regained consciousness while the coaches were helping me into a car. I saw Dan standing by the shotput circle, looking sad and concerned. I waved at him and tried to yell, "It's okay! Don't worry!" I didn't know if my voice was strong enough for him to hear and understand.

There was something positive that resulted from this experience. Now I was that young square-built sophomore boy with a long, shaved patch on his head and 17 angry-looking stitches. Those stitches could be used at school to attract attention from the girls. It was totally worth it!

These stories are a reminder of the risks and dangers many of us have experienced, and yet, amazingly, we have survived, largely because others have come to our rescue.

The author of the Psalms writes, "...you knit me together in my mother's womb. I praise you because I am fearfully and wonderfully made."

We are perfectly formed with resilience and intelligence;

resilience enough to withstand most of the dangers we face, yet intelligent enough to know we can't survive on our own. We need each other.

And, even with the help of those who care about us, it is nothing short of a miracle that we have made it to adulthood.

> "It's not about how fast you run or how high you climb, but how well you bounce."
>
> - Tigger (A.A. Milne)

42
If I Could Turn Back Time

If you could turn back time, what would you do differently? Would you buy a different house or car? Choose another career? Invest in that risky but potentially lucrative stock? Pick a different life partner. Retire sooner? Later? I'd have to answer no to all of those questions.

Would you take back any words or actions if you could? Conversely, were there times when you wish you'd said or done something that you didn't? Unfortunately, I'd have to answer yes.

"Regrets, I've had a few," Frank Sinatra crooned. We've probably all had some regrets at one time or another.

If I could turn back time, I'd try harder to stay in touch with my father. I was four when my parents separated. We moved back to Wisconsin, where my mom grew up, and he stayed in

Florida. He died when I was 11. So, it's not like it was completely within my power to stay in touch with him, considering my age and the distance between us. But I could have done better.

My dad and I exchanged letters when I was barely old enough to write. He always answered the letters I wrote to him, but then I quit writing. I'm not sure why. Even though I was the one who ended our correspondence, it was always my dream to grow up and find him so I could show him how well I turned out. But I never had the chance.

Another regret: I wish I'd asked my mother more questions about her life. As I mentioned in a previous chapter, I realized when I started writing Mom's story, *Betty: A Memoir*, that there was so much about her I didn't know, and I had waited too long to ask her. I think Mom would have been flattered that I was interested in her life, and she would have been happy to answer any and all of my questions.

But we were busy with our lives, raising kids, and trying to make ends meet. Then we had grandkids, and traveling to visit them kept us on the road a lot. So many excuses not to take the time.

After Mom's terminal diagnosis, my sister and I had plenty of time to ask all the questions we wanted to. But I didn't want to tire her with questions like, "Did you and your mom get along when you were young? Did you love my dad? Did you love any other man before or after he died?" Plus, I didn't want to take the chance that my questions would make her sad.

You've heard it said that hindsight is 20/20. But is it? Knowing what I know now, would I do things differently? Or would I avoid the hard things by using the excuse that "things always turn out the way they were meant to?" It's hard to say.

For example, who remembers 2020 and Covid-19? Hard to forget, right? If the virus didn't change your life in some way, at least temporarily, then you're probably in the minority.

You most likely lined up for COVID-19 shots or, at the very least, wore a mask during the year. Schools closed temporarily, restaurants offered only drive-up service, theatres went dark, and weddings and other large events were canceled. Many people couldn't visit extended family or nursing home residents because they were told they should quarantine. It was a strange time.

I remember when I first heard the media report about Covid and how it could have a major effect on the world's health. I pooh-poohed the dire predictions. We had all lived through viruses and rumors of viruses that turned out to be nothing.

Covid hit older or frail people the hardest. Many died. Then we started hearing reports of people younger than we are who were being admitted to the ICU, even in our small town of about 10,000.

Steve and I started taking the warnings more seriously. We made sure to get all of the shots, and we wore masks when and where they were required. We strongly encouraged our children and grandchildren to do so, as well.

But, on the other hand, we went south for two months against the advice of health professionals that people should curtail travel. As mask restrictions were lifted, we didn't wear them. Too confining. (Didn't people also say that about seatbelts back in the '60s?)

Despite our somewhat lax attitude regarding masks and quarantine, we didn't get Covid. But we know people who took the same precautions we did—shots, avoiding crowds, and wearing masks where required—but despite their precautions, they got Covid anyway, and some contracted the virus more than once.

Knowing what we know now, I'm not sure we'd change anything we did (or didn't do) to avoid Covid. We were cautious but not obsessive. We must have done something right. Or maybe it was just dumb luck.

It's a moot point since none of us can turn back time. Maybe it would be more productive to think about what we **could** do today that our future selves will thank us for.

One of my close friends recently gave us this advice: "If there's something you want to do, DO IT NOW!" She didn't have to explain. It was based on personal experience. Her husband had a stroke several months ago, which has limited his mobility, and some of their plans for retirement had to be put on hold or canceled.

Another close friend lost her husband a year and a half ago. Before he died, he told us that they were both so glad they'd taken a trip to Alaska with their kids and grandkids the previous year while he was still healthy.

Our friends' advice has become our mantra. We are retired, in good health, and in fairly good physical condition. If there's something we want to do, we won't put it off for some time in the future, not knowing how long "our future" will last.

To celebrate our 50th wedding anniversary, we took our three children and their spouses on an Alaskan cruise in 2021. It was a wonderful experience for all of us. We go south every winter to enjoy warm weather on the Gulf instead of staying in Northwest Iowa and shoveling snow. Next week, we'll be flying to New York City to see the sites and attend a Broadway show with two of our college-age grandsons. We took their older brothers to NYC a couple of years ago.

Celebrating our 50th with our children on the cruise ship.

It's not without some apprehension that we do these trips—we are still small-town rural kids at heart. But after a successful trip, the time spent with grandkids and the memories made are worth the pre-travel anxiety.

You don't have to be retired or spending your children's inheritance to live by the maxim: *Do today what your future selves will thank you for.*

Another motto to consider: *Do it now! Sometimes "later" becomes "never."*

And in the words of Willie Nelson: "A*in't it funny how time slips away...?"*

If I Could Turn Back Time

The view from our ship docked at Juneau, Alaska.

43

But That Was Yesterday, and Yesterday's Gone

The 1985 song by Foreigner, *That Was Yesterday,* is about a failed relationship the writer is clinging to in the hope that there is a chance it could still be saved.

I feel a spark of regret when I hear that song. When reminiscing about our past, we sometimes say, "But that was yesterday, and yesterday's gone." Many of those trips down memory lane are about things we used to do that we can't do anymore.

Regardless of our current age, there is a sense of wistfulness inside many of us when we remember the younger version of ourselves. That keeps us hoping we might somehow go back to the time when our bodies were agile and strong. But when we look in the mirror, the reality of age hits us in the face and leaves wrinkles in its path.

But That Was Yesterday, and Yesterday's Gone

Time has powerful allies, including genes that control hormones, causing gradual changes in muscle development, energy levels, and even temperament. Those changes slow us down; we exercise less, lose muscle, and eat more of what we know as comfort foods that aren't always good for our bodies.

As a Health and Physical Education major who also coached, I'd like to share some of the strategies that have worked for me in my life.

And by "worked for me," I mean that I am almost 72, happy and healthy. I have lost some unwanted pounds over the last couple of years. I'm still able to do most of the activities I've always done and want or need to do, though not at the level I was able to in my younger days. It is my hope that some of this is useful for you.

The medical term for degenerative loss of muscle due to aging or immobility is s*arcopenia*. Starting at about age 30, we lose as much as 3% to 5% of muscle mass every decade. Most men will lose about 30% of their muscle mass in a 90-year lifetime. Women have a greater rate of loss in general, as much as 8% each decade, and about a 48% loss of muscle mass over six decades.

We can, however, slow down the process and stay stronger longer in order to more fully enjoy our golden years. Here are some tried and true strategies suggested by experts gleaned from research on aging.

Strength training can help build muscle, make you stronger, increase your endurance, and make everyday activities easier and safer. Try to do strength training exercises two days a week.

Start with exercise bands or light hand weights, and as you

gain strength, graduate to weight machines or even free weights. My mother-in-law lifted cans of vegetables from her cupboard because she didn't have dumbbells. Every object has weight regardless of its shape.

Yoga is highly recommended for seniors. It promotes flexibility and helps to improve strength and balance, which also adds a margin of safety to your life as you age.

According to an article published by Harvard Medical School, yoga, with its emphasis on breath and meditation, both of which calm and center the mind, also brings mental health benefits, such as reduced anxiety, stress, and depression. Yoga also strengthens parts of the brain that play a key role in memory, attention, awareness, thought, and language.

Swimming is a wonderful exercise for anyone, but especially those over 60. It's a low-impact activity that improves muscular strength as well as heart and circulatory health.

Strength training, yoga, and swimming are exercise activities that usually require a specialized location, instruction, and/or equipment. But you can get similarly healthy results on your own too.

Begin by thinking about what you want your life to be like now and in the future. If you want to travel, for example, then you will need to walk in airports while handling a suitcase. So, try walking around the house or outside carrying a bag with five pounds of weight inside.

I personally enjoy camping. There are parts and attachments on and under our little camper that need to be checked and tightened. Hitching to our Durango is a bit tricky with some squatting and sometimes lifting the hitch. I need to be able to crawl under the camper at times to open and close valves. It requires flexibility and strength, but it is also great exercise.

Here are some other practical ideas:

I often say, *"We need to keep on going so we can keep on going."* In its most basic form, exercise is simply using our muscles to get moving and keep on moving. So, let's MOVE!

Doctors tell us we should do 30 to 40 minutes of brisk walking, cycling, swimming, dancing, or nature walks each day. That would be ideal, and it certainly is achievable for most people, but not for everyone. For those who have limited mobility, remember that doing something is better than doing nothing when it comes to exercise.

Little things can make a difference. For example, standing is better than sitting. My Apple watch vibrates every hour, reminding me to stand if I have been sitting too long, and it lets me know when I've achieved my exercise goals for the day. Move as much as you can, even if you are limited in what you can do safely.

Count your chores as exercise. Mowing the lawn with a push mower, as opposed to a riding mower, is great exercise. So is carrying a laundry basket, folding clothes, vacuuming, mopping floors, and shopping.

Apply this same concept to all the work you do around the house. Instead of avoiding a chore or feeling like your time isn't being well spent, get in the mindset of appreciating what it does for your physical and emotional health.

Climbing stairs is hard work, but in order to be able to climb stairs as we age, we need to do it now.

We worried about my 90-year-old mother, who didn't want to move from her second-floor apartment. She was not able to go down the stairs by herself, which was one of the requirements to live in the building. We gently asked what she would do if there was a fire and she couldn't use the elevator.

It turns out she had a strategy. She told us she would sit down on the top step and scoot herself down each step to the bottom. Problem solved, she thought.

"But Mom, when you get to the bottom of the steps, can you get back up off the floor by yourself?" I asked.

Tearfully she admitted that she couldn't. It's good that she had a plan, but there were so many things that could go wrong with her plan.

If you have stairs in your house, use them often. Consider passing up the elevator in a public building if you're just going one or two floors, or take the elevator going up and the stairs coming down.

Stairs are not for wimps. Mary and I took our grandsons, Jack and Tim, to New York City as a graduation gift to see a Broadway show and tour the city. On our first morning there, we were looking forward to breakfast in the café on the main floor.

The elevator was taking too long, so we decided to take the stairs down instead. How hard can it be to walk down 32 flights of stairs? You have gravity on your side, right?

The next morning, Mary could barely walk, and I moved very slowly. We tried to hide our discomfort from the grandsons, but they probably wondered why we weren't keeping up with them. The stair marathon didn't seem to have any negative effect on the youngsters.

If you're not interested in yoga, you can work on balance and agility on your own. I challenge you to dress and undress while standing. But do it safely to avoid falls—stand close to a piece of furniture or a wall so you can lean against it if you start to lose your balance. You may find that it's harder to do than it sounds.

Make it a life habit to exercise daily. This is not lost time. It is gained time in the long run. It's easier if you put exercise on your schedule for the same time every day.

I find being outdoors is the most interesting way to maintain a moderate exercise plan. The air is fresh, and the views can be stunning—certainly better than the four walls in a house. I don't exercise outside when the temperature with wind chill hits zero.

As a track coach, I learned to enjoy running with my girls' track team. I got to the point where I could run four or five miles comfortably each morning before school, which I did for 30 years. I eventually started having back pain and a heart rhythm issue which forced me to rethink my healthy lifestyle plan.

So, I switched from running to biking. Now I ride my bike all year round at 5:30 or 6:00 each morning. I ride pre-timed routes in town so that I achieve my goal of biking 40-60 minutes daily.

You might be wondering about biking in the winter in Northwest Iowa. I have a second bike with wide "fat" tires that work well in the snow and on crunchy ice. However, there is no tire that works well on smooth, glassy ice, so on those days, I don't ride. When we go south for two months in the winter, we pack our bikes.

If you decide to try winter biking, I'd recommend you wait until the snowplows have been out. They go fast, and I don't like to ride in front of them. It could give new meaning to the phrase "getting plowed."

While I ride, I take a lot of sunrise and low-light pictures. It is often an amazing experience. I get some beautiful photos, and that's another reward for exercising.

After my bike ride, I do stretches, sit-ups, and push-ups in our driveway, sometimes giving a start to the occasional walker going by. While resting quietly for a few minutes between exercise sets on a cold morning, I heard a woman ask her walking partner, "Is he dead?"

Another reason to keep moving!

A couple photos from my daily bike rides. Mary and I stopped to mark the moment when my bike computer logged 10,000 miles.

44
In My Heart You Will Remain Forever Young

It has been fun, and sometimes challenging, to come up with an appropriate title that accurately sums up the theme for each episode. You may have noticed that we've used song titles or lyrics for all chapter titles, including this one (Sometimes we put our own spin on them. Our apologies to the songwriters.)

My first thought when I considered "Forever Young" was: "Well, that's false advertising! No one can stay young forever. What was Bob Dylan thinking when he wrote those lyrics? What did he mean by that bold statement?"

So, I put on my newspaper reporter hat (after brushing off 30+ years of dust), and I did some research on the meaning behind the lyrics. Dylan wrote two versions of the song for each of his young sons—one a lullaby and one in more of a rock style.

It was Dylan's hope that his sons would stay forever young at heart, growing up to be strong and happy, always trying new things. He urged them to never give up and to live life to its fullest.

Okay, now I get it, and I concur. Those qualities, lifestyles, and attitudes, along with exercise, diet, and good genes, keep us young at heart throughout the inevitable aging process.

In our last chapter, "But That Was Yesterday...And Yesterday's Gone," Steve wrote about the importance of exercise as we age, based on his education in health and physical fitness and his coaching experience. In this chapter, I will touch on additional factors, including diet, lifestyle, attitudes, and genetics.

Full disclosure: I'm not an expert, or anything close to an expert, in any of those areas. Feel free to fact-check me on anything I've written here. And let me know if you've found evidence to disprove any of my comments.

First, let's get **genetics** out of the way. There's really nothing we can do about our genes except marry well so that we pass good genes on to our children. It's too late for us, and I doubt young folks will insist that their potential mates have a 23andMe test before they pop the question.

On to No. 2: **The Dreaded Diet.**

For me, lecturing anyone on diet would be like the pot calling the kettle black. Or maybe like the pot calling the shiny new stainless-steel pan black if you have been making healthy eating a priority your whole life.

My diet and weight management history has been erratic and downright dismal, especially when we had young children and were on a tight budget. But Steve and I have learned a few things about nutrition and weight loss along the way, so I'll skip over my early years and write about what has worked for us in the last three years.

In 2020, the year we both turned 69, we decided it was time to get serious about our health and get rid of the extra pounds we'd been carrying around. So we developed a nutritionally balanced meal plan based on current recommendations and our food preferences that we thought we could stick to for at least a year and, hopefully, a lifetime. So here it is in a nutshell:

We have a **high protein, low carbohydrate breakfast** consisting of a piece of whole wheat toast and peanut butter (although it's high in calories, it's also high in protein, and, bottom line, we like it); then we layer it with flavored Greek yogurt; and finally, we top that off with berries or ½ of a sliced banana. Sometimes we skip the toast and peanut butter and just have Greek yogurt with berries on top, or we have a bowl of oatmeal with almond milk. Steel-cut oatmeal has the most fiber but takes longer to cook. The solution: Mix the oats and milk in a bowl the night before, keep in the refrigerator, and you'll find it's ready in half the cooking time.

Lunch is a large green salad topped with lots of raw vegetables and some protein, usually chicken, shrimp, or black beans, with a low-calorie dressing. I make my own dressing with any flavor of sugar-free Greek yogurt and light raspberry dressing.

Our evening meal is more varied. It might be egg-white omelets, whole wheat pasta or riced cauliflower with spaghetti sauce, a rotisserie chicken sandwich on whole wheat bread, or homemade soup. We make it in a big crockpot and put leftovers in freezer/microwave-safe glass containers.

Occasionally, we have pizza or burgers (once again, because we like those foods, and they help us to enjoy our eating plan.) We try to limit, not always successfully, our intake of sugar, red meat, most dairy, and unhealthy oils that are high in saturated fat.

In answer to your first question: We have been pleasantly surprised to discover that, although we don't have much variety in daily menus, the meals aren't boring. In fact, we think that the routine helps us stick to our eating plan and requires a smaller variety of groceries to have on hand.

Another bonus of repeating the same menus is the simplicity of the routine. We don't spend a lot of time menu planning because we know what food items will be on our shopping list, and we almost always know what our next meal will be. As a result, we seldom ask, "What shall we have for breakfast/lunch/dinner?"

While traveling, on special occasions, or if we go out to eat with friends, we often order a meal that isn't low-calorie or all that nutritious. But we don't turn down invitations with friends even if it means we may stray from our daily calorie goals. Instead, we justify going out to eat by always sharing a restaurant meal, which cuts our calories in half.

For the record: We are not health nuts, and cutting back isn't always easy for us. Steve has said that in his perfect imaginary world, his diet would be white bread, pizza, brownies, pie, ice cream, buttered mashed potatoes with gravy, and coffee. I think I could live on pizza and ice cream for lunch and dinner. And for breakfast? Breakfast pizza, of course.

Although our eating plan isn't perfect, Steve lost 30 lbs., and I lost 40 lbs. in 2020. We're still not where we'd like to be, but we're a lot closer. We continue to stay on our "diet" because it is fairly healthy, and our bodies have gotten used to the routine of repeating menus, making it easier for us to stay with it.

The benefits of losing weight have been our reward for limiting certain foods and calories. Everything is easier, from getting dressed in the morning to going for a walk in the afternoon. Our annual blood screen results, though not perfect, are proof that we're doing something right.

When we took two of our grandsons, ages 19 and 20, to New York City last week for four days, we walked 29.8 miles. I don't think I could have walked anywhere near that far when I was 40 lbs. heavier. I would have had to sit in our hotel room, missing some of our best adventures. We also ate pizza for almost every meal (we let them choose the restaurants), so hopefully, all that walking canceled out the calories. (If only.)

Here are just a few activities and behaviors that can keep all of us young, regardless of our current age:

- **Try new things**, even if they're a little scary. Travel to places you've never been before. While in NYC with Sam and Charlie, we worked up the nerve to ride the subway. We took the train from Penn Station to Wall Street, where we boarded the Staten Island Ferry. Deciding to experience the subway took more courage than anything I've done in the last decade—except maybe a few scary taxi rides from LaGuardia to downtown.
- **Learn new things**. If you don't know all the potential uses that a laptop or cell phone have to offer you, ask a child or grandchild for help. Check out course offerings (credit or non-credit) at your local community college to learn more about everything from technology to cooking to gardening.
- Did you **play a musical instrument** in high school? Pick it up and start playing again. Since Steve started playing baritone again, his playing has dramatically improved! Several times during the summer and again

over the Christmas holidays he plays in community concerts.
- What **hobbies** did you have when you were younger but have since abandoned? Drawing, painting, crafting, quilting? How about trying them again? For me, it's writing. Retirement has given me the time to write again, something I have missed but thoroughly enjoy.
- Engage in **daily activities that stimulate your brain**: Do word puzzles or math problems, read books or e-books, put puzzles together, solve a Rubik's cube, or play difficult board and card games.
- **Listen to music.** It will stimulate your brain and may lower your blood pressure.
- **Maintain a positive attitude.** Be thankful for what you have.
- **Volunteer.** Serving others and feeling needed and useful will help you feel better about yourself, your community, and the world.

Although Dylan wrote "Forever Young" for his children, I think the lyrics apply to the rest of us, regardless of age. If you're curious to learn more about Dylan or the lyrics of the song or about any other topic, google it—another activity that will stimulate your brain and help you learn something new.

45
Words Get in the Way

"Look up in the sky! It's a bird! It's a plane! It's Superman! Who, disguised as Clark Kent, mild-mannered reporter for a great metropolitan newspaper, fights a never-ending battle for truth, justice, and the American Way."

Millions listened to these familiar words that began each episode of *The Adventures of Superman*, which aired between 1951 and 1958 and starred George Reeves. As a kid, I was fascinated with the description of this character who was strong enough to conquer evil and never used his superhuman abilities to take advantage of people.

As I watched the show, I wondered what it would be like to fly. I even tried it a few times. I crashed a lot.

I didn't know at the time that the comic book character was created and published in 1938 during the last years of the Great Depression. After nearly a decade of hardship for most of the population, Superman was a spark of hope cutting through the darkness of the prevailing feelings of discouragement and defeat. Those words from the Superman introduction were especially powerful because the years of the Depression called for strong leaders who consistently stood for truth and justice.

We often write, read, or speak words without considering the real meaning or the power the words might have on others. The catchphrase, "The American Way," has puzzled me over the years. I've come to the conclusion that, although it sounds good, it means different things to different people.

The America I was born into gave me a good education. I found the love of my life and provided for my family through a fulfilling career. We have a wonderful marriage and three happy, well-adjusted children who met and married amazing partners. They have given us ten beautiful and talented grandchildren who have brought us joy.

On the other hand, a woman living in a car or homeless shelter with her children because she can't afford rent would likely have a different perspective on the American Way. I'm sure her description would contrast with mine. A young black man born and raised in the projects of Saint Louis will no doubt see a different America.

Some might describe the American Way in terms of the strength of its military, its system of government, the sustainability of its economy, or its influence in the world. Idealistic citizens might refer to the freedom or liberty found here.

But what do we mean when using words like "truth and justice" or "freedom and liberty?" More importantly, do we believe in them enough to change how we do business and live our daily lives? Do we want everyone to experience truth,

Words Get in the Way

justice, freedom, and liberty equally?

Mary and I have shared about our recent trip to New York City with two of our grandsons. Included on our list of must-do things (besides a Broadway show and pizza) was to go to the south end of Manhattan to see the Statue of Liberty, the 9/11 memorial, the Freedom Tower, and Trinity Church, where Alexander Hamilton, his wife Eliza, and son Phillip are buried. These historical sites forced us to think about the lives given to defend freedom and for the blessings we have because we live in America.

While walking around the 9/11 memorial, I looked for familiar names engraved into the granite, pondering the depth of pain and loss represented there. The huge, seemingly bottomless square hole with water flowing down its sides symbolized to me the way the world uses up people's lives every day for causes that are—or are sometimes imagined to be—great.

While moving among the crowds near the memorial, there is a solemn, meditative atmosphere that contrasts with much of the loud and busy city. So many everyday working people died in this place. Many lives were lost because they were simply in the wrong place at the wrong time, but some chose to run into harm's way to rescue others in danger.

These deaths occurred because six men who were raised in a completely different environment were convinced by a religious fanatic's words that they should kill Americans. They were told that, by carrying out these horrific acts, they would be rewarded with eternal happiness, riches, and many wives.

From the 9/11 memorial, we took the Staten Island Ferry and slowly cruised by the Statue of Liberty. The words engraved on the base of the statue are sobering and unforgettable:

"Give me your tired, your poor, your huddled masses yearning to breathe free, the wretched refuse of your teeming shore."

What a wonderful, generous, loving, and Christian ideal. I wonder if Americans truly believe and act on these words. Do we welcome the huddled masses yearning to breathe free? Or do we selfishly refuse to share our resources?

Recognizing the value that the words "liberty" and "freedom" have for people who haven't had the luxury of living without discrimination, poverty, and corrupt leadership helps us understand why "the tired, the poor" from "teeming shores" are trying so desperately to come here. It shouldn't surprise us. Wouldn't we do the same if our families were at great risk?

I was filled with a feeling of pride as we sailed by Lady Liberty. Seeing her in the harbor caused me to wonder what the immigrants from years past felt as they arrived at Ellis Island—some of my relatives and maybe yours. What excitement that sight must have generated!

Statues and monuments, like the 9/11 Memorial, can have the same influence as words. They remind us of dreams that others before us strived for, the pain of loss, or the joy of victory in the struggle to achieve those highest goals. Hearts full of love, concern, empathy, and understanding bring change to the thoughts, values, and actions of others.

The Freedom Tower is a gigantic, starkly crystalline affirmation that this country will not be intimidated by the evil actions of a few. As I stood looking up to the top, I could almost see and feel the defiance in the faces of those who hate us because we are Americans. The world is a complex place, but even so, we need to ask ourselves why there is so much animosity toward this country, and we need to ask what we can do to make life better for all people.

St. Patrick's Cathedral was another highlight for us. It's like the Freedom Tower but in a different realm. As we looked across 5th Avenue, walking toward the cathedral, we saw a large statue of Atlas carrying the world on his shoulders. From our perspective, Atlas is dwarfed by the cathedral, symbolizing a place where God dwells. Atlas, the "Superman" of the ancient myths, is but a speck compared to the God who created the universe.

If we had taken a helicopter ride over the city, we would have been able to see that the cathedral is built in the shape of a cross, the paradoxical symbol of a God who loves us and wants to save us through sacrifice. God gave his Son for us, not wanting to reign above us but live in us; not satisfied to dwell in temples of stone but longing to live in the "temples of our hearts."

For the good of our country, our neighbors, and even our faith, I suggest we implement God's plan for developing people and relationships that is expressed in the words *sacrifice, love, service, giving, and sharing,* for starters. I would like to be able to say these words describe the American Way.

This quote sums up in a few words what I am attempting to express:

"My task which I am trying to achieve is, by the power of the written word, to make you hear, to make you feel—it is, before all, to make you see... If I succeed, you shall perhaps find that glimpse of truth for which you have forgotten to ask." ~ Joseph Conrad, Polish-born English novelist

As we walked away from St. Patrick's Cathedral, a glance back reveals Atlas carrying the world on his shoulders, juxtaposed with the towering cathedral.

46

Teach Your Children Well

Steve and I were married young by today's standards—we were not quite 20 and became parents two years later, at not quite 22, when we had our first child, Joe. Aaron joined the family 20 months later, and Laura arrived 26 months after Aaron.

All this to say that we were young and dumb when we were married and even less prepared to have children. In a way, being so naïve was an advantage because we didn't understand that raising children was a far greater responsibility than we could imagine. We also didn't know how disastrous the repercussions might be if we failed miserably.

And so, I am pleased to share with you that, despite having young and dumb parents, none of our kids are on the FBI Most Wanted List. (We set the bar fairly low.)

Now that we're older, we realize how lucky we were. "Blessed" is perhaps a more accurate term. Our kids have grown up to be productive citizens who, along with their spouses, are exemplary parents to their own children.

Still, we can't help but wonder if we taught them all they needed to know during the 18 years or so when we had the best chance of influencing them. Our lives were busy with our jobs; feeding, clothing, and educating our kids; and trying to make ends meet on meager paychecks and virtually no savings. I don't remember that we gave a lot of thought to what we wanted our children to learn from us.

So now, almost 50 years after the birth of our first child, we've compiled a list of the traits, attitudes, and behaviors we hope our kids learned through our examples, words, and actions. We also gave a great deal of thought to identifying what we've learned from them. A few of our friends shared their wisdom as well.

This is not an all-inclusive list, but it encompasses some of what we think are the most important lessons to teach children:

Be friendly. Greet people when you step onto an elevator full of strangers or in a checkout line. Compliment a service worker. Look people in the eye when you talk to them. Really listen to what they are saying instead of thinking ahead about how you will respond.

My longtime friend Millie would add: Treat people as you would like to be treated.

Margo, another "old" friend, said of her daughter, "She is kinder and more generous than I am, but I hope she got some of it from me." Margo's husband, Tom, added that he tried to teach their children to be patient and that they taught him to be more patient as he got older. A full circle.

Always, always use good manners. Say please and thank you. Write thank you notes or emails for gifts or special acts of kindness shown to you. Hold the door open for someone else. These are all simple things we learned early in life, but we often get too busy or we forget to do them.

When I asked my friend, Jane, what she hoped she had taught her children, the first thing she mentioned was that her daughter, Clare, "has excellent manners." Lori, a friend of Jane's, agreed: "Clare is kind and loving. She makes me feel like more than her mom's friend—I feel that she is really interested in me as a person."

None of this surprises me. Children learn by watching their parents as well as by listening to them. Clare is exactly like her mother.

Be honest, responsible, trustworthy, and humble. Keep your promises. Millie says they taught their boys, "If you say you're going to do something, then do it." Several parents said they taught their children the importance of always telling the truth and apologizing immediately when they're in the wrong.

Be compassionate and generous. Tip your waiter. Give to charities you know are making a difference. If you see a person on the street with a cardboard sign and a tin cup, give him a few bucks. Yes, it's possible he or she will spend it on drugs, or he/she might be scamming you. Maybe that person could get a job instead of asking for a handout. But take the risk, hoping the money will be used to buy a much-needed meal, coat, or help pay for rent.

I was in Chicago a few years ago for a meeting with my work peers who were from all over the country. We were at a fast-food restaurant, waiting for our order when a woman came up to us and asked for money to buy food for her family. Just guessing from her behavior, I'd say she either had mental health issues or she was high. I gave her some cash. The others chided me, saying she would probably use my money to buy drugs. I agreed that it might have been better if I had just bought some food for her or given her a gift card for a fast-food restaurant.

After eating, the others returned to our hotel, but I decided to tour the city on foot for a while. After walking just a few blocks, I was hopelessly lost. (Have I mentioned that I have absolutely no sense of direction?) It was starting to get dark. Just when I was about to panic, I saw a familiar face. Not a co-worker, but the woman to whom I had given a few bucks.

She asked me for money again. I told her I'd just given her money at the restaurant. Then I asked her if she could tell me how to get back to my hotel. She not only knew where it was, but she insisted on walking me all the way to the front door.

I took a risk following her, but I was thankful I had. (Or I still might be wandering around Chicago.) The incident reminded me of the words: *Cast your bread upon the waters...* (Ecclesiastes 11:1). Getting something in return should not be our motive for doing good, but it's often a result. Pay it forward!

Leave a place better than you found it. If you use something, put it back where it belongs. But don't just pick up after yourself. If you see a piece of clothing that has been knocked down onto the floor of a clothing store, hang it up. Yes, I know it's not your job and that people are hired to keep the store tidy, but the whole point is to go the extra mile.

Leave people feeling better than when you found them. Even a brief conversation in which you do most of the listening might be what a lonely, grieving, anxious, or angry person needs. Maybe words aren't always necessary—sometimes, just a smile would help.

Love your neighbor. The Question: Who is my neighbor? The Answer: Anyone anywhere in the world who is not me.

Remember that your neighbor isn't just the person who lives next door. He or she might be Muslim, Hispanic, African American, Asian, Gay, Lesbian, Transgender, or an Atheist. They may belong to a different political party, have a lower economic or educational status, be from another country or culture, or have mental health issues. If you say you love your neighbor but don't want them in your neighborhood, you've missed the point. You don't have to agree with them or even understand them, but love them anyway.

My mother was a believer but not a consistent churchgoer. (That may sound like an oxymoron, but it would take several chapters for me to explain the statement.) Mom worked in Saudi Arabia for several years as a nurse in a huge hospital where the staff included people from nearly every country in the world.

When she returned to the U.S., Mom often heard derogatory comments about Muslims. Sometimes people would use the words "Muslims" and "terrorists" interchangeably. Mom was quick to point out that the Muslims she'd met were some of the kindest, most generous, and most compassionate people she'd ever known.

Without ever telling me how I should feel about people who were different than we were, she impressed upon me the importance of refraining from stereotyping and judging others by their religion or the color of their skin.

I think a quote on the garden stone that my sister, Susan,

gave me says it well:

"Just love everybody. I'll sort them out later." – God

Art print by Bryan Andreas, courtesy of StoryPeople, Decorah, IA

Make worship a priority. Our children have continued to grow in their faith, and they make worship a priority with their families. I think they also learned that worship is not just a Sunday morning activity; it doesn't just occur inside a white sided or red brick building with a pastor and a praise-and-worship team. Worship is also when you practice the traits and attitudes we've mentioned: kindness, generosity, compassion, and being friendly—all of which make the world a better place.

All that said, here's the best advice we can give you as parents:

> *"The most important thing a father can do for his children is love their mother." — Unknown*

So, what did we, as parents, learn from our children?

Margo said their grown children taught them the importance of exercise as they age. They have taken their kids' advice.

Steve says he learned to discipline our children differently than his father. He discovered that a discussion without anger was more effective and productive when our kids broke the rules. "Sometimes it's best not to make too much of an incident and to keep a sense of humor during those discussions," he added.

One last thought: No matter how well you teach your children, they will learn from others. Sometimes that can be a good thing. For example, our children participated in Fellowship of Christian Athletes, led by excellent teachers who were also coaches. They positively affected our kids' attitudes and behaviors, and we are grateful for their part in influencing them to make good choices.

Sometimes learning from others can be detrimental to molding a child's character, as in this memory from 40+ years ago:

Steve and I never used profanity and were especially careful to watch our language in our children's presence. Our oldest child, Joe, was a happy and carefree kid, rarely breaking our rules. When he was about eight, he and Steve were throwing a frisbee back and forth in our front yard. After an especially nice toss, helped by a breeze, the frisbee sailed high over Steve's head.

Joe, excited about his best frisbee toss ever, joyfully and innocently said, "That thing flies like hell, doesn't it, Dad?"

Joe, Aaron, and Dave with their sons, Trevor, Rowan, and Benjamin.

47

Teach Your Grandchildren Well

I read a story in the AARP Magazine about a young man, Brad, who asked his grandmother, Joy, to go on a "grand adventure" with him. She had never seen mountains or slept in a tent but immediately agreed to be her grandson's camping and traveling buddy.

That single trip to the Great Smoky Mountains National Park eight years ago evolved into a quest to visit all 63 national parks together. During those camping trips, Grandma Joy climbed a mountain at the age of 85 and went white water rafting at 93. The two will complete their tour when they visit American Samoa soon. (Joy and Brad have visited all national parks since this writing.)

"We found out how much we needed each other and needed this kind of adventure," Brad said. "We've spent so many hours together that she's been able to give me her wisdom and show me what resilience looks like."

What else has he learned from his grandma? "I've learned that I have to do the things I love while I still have good knees!"

Joy's words are great advice for all of us: "Don't worry about the small stuff... You need to be optimistic about everything... If you have the strength to get out of bed, get up and enjoy it!"

What an admirable example of the bond that exists between the two generations. I am in awe of a grandmother willing to take risks and experience new adventures, but I'm also touched that this grandson was willing and eager to travel so many miles with an 85-year-old woman.

In my last chapter (with a little help from our friends), I wrote about what we hope we've taught our kids and what we've learned from them. Many of those same lessons apply to grandchildren. Chapter 33 is an open letter to my grandchildren, so if I've repeated myself, it's because it bears repeating. (Plus, I'm getting old, and my memory is fading fast.)

If you're a grandparent, you probably remember the moment when your first grandchild was placed in your arms—the excitement, the joy, and the instantaneous love you felt for that tiny baby. You probably also felt a strong desire to be a good role model for this little one and all future grandchildren with whom you may be blessed.

My friend, Lorelei, experienced those feelings when she became a first-time grandmother just two weeks ago. She said she hopes to be a good Christian example, kind and thoughtful, for her granddaughter. Lorelei added, "...I think sometimes children listen to their grandparents better than their parents."

I agree. But why is that?

Is it because grandparents, especially those who are retired, often have more time to spend with their grandchildren? Is it because grandkids have been taught to be kind and respectful to older people in general? Or could it be that since grandparents don't have to worry about the family budget, jobs, or busy schedules and aren't responsible for discipline, they can be more relaxed with their grandchildren? Maybe all of the above.

I think another factor might be that this is a second chance for grandparents to "get it right." Steve and I weren't perfect parents—there are many moments in our child-raising years that we wish we could rewind and do over. I think it's safe to say we're better grandparents than we were parents.

Lora and Gary said they try to give their grandchildren the time, attention, and unconditional love children crave and prefer over material things. "That is what bonds us and builds a trusting relationship," they said.

Our friends who shared their thoughts on grandparenting with us agreed that how we live our lives strongly influences our grandchildren.

"Be the person you want them to become," Julie said. "Walk the talk."

Linda said, "Teach them, by example, kindness, forgiveness, acceptance, and the importance of family. Always tell them they are loved and reinforce Jesus's love for them." She said it's also important that grandkids know that "at Grandma's house, we have fun together."

Kids today may be worrying about grades, pressure to perform in athletics, their parent's approval, and peer pressure. They need to know there's a place where they can go to relax, de-stress, and just have fun.

The grandparents also emphasized character building. "The thing I hear myself telling my grandkids repeatedly is that doing the *'right'* thing isn't always the *easy* thing," Mary Ann said. She added that she enjoys watching her grandkids participate in athletic events "when they're put into the game for two minutes or when they're starters," which she couldn't always do when her own kids were on the bench.

The same applies to athletics. "I'm just as proud of them for getting a B as an A. None of that matters. I see them more like God sees them. What's most important is being a good human," Mary Ann added.

Steve said, "Grandparents have experienced, in a broader sense, what it means for children to be 'successful.' Parents tend to think more competitively about their children's success and achievement in the short term by comparing their kids with other children."

I hope my grandchildren have learned the qualities that contribute to being a good human: serve others through service opportunities; defend those who can't defend themselves; cherish your family and make an effort to stay close to them; don't stereotype or judge others by the color of their skin, religion, culture, gender, age... In a nutshell: Don't judge. Period.

I also hope our grandkids have learned to follow their dreams regardless of roadblocks that may get in the way. Sometimes their dreams and goals will change. That's okay. I hope they will be open to new ideas and opportunities, even if it means switching majors or careers, switching colleges, or dropping out if they think that makes sense for them.

We knew that once our grandchildren went off to college and, as in the case of our oldest grandson, got married, it would be difficult to continue the tradition of spending large blocks of time with them like we had done when they were younger through Christmas Adventures. We will have to look for new ways to strengthen our bond.

All 10 of our grandchildren live within a five-hour drive of our home, except for two in college in Indiana. But not all grandparents have the luxury of living near their grandchildren. Mary and Tim have two grandkids who live nearby, but their other three grandchildren lived 6,000 miles away for seven years.

"We could do sleepovers, field trips, cooking, and crafting with our grandkids who are close, but building relationships with the Middle East group was more challenging. Also, mail was not dependable, and the kids didn't have phones, so we couldn't text." Instead, Mary said they talked weekly using FaceTime and a special app to make video messages.

"I read books to them via FaceTime—picture books at first and then chapter books, one chapter at a time...Once, we made my potato soup over FaceTime ... Sometimes we even played dice games like Yahtzee and Farkle."

Mary and Tim could visit the distant grandkids just once a year, but they stayed for two to three weeks and were able to spend every day with the grandkids. "Grandparenting is a joy no matter where you or your grandchildren live," Mary said.

Our friends Margo and Tom shared this sweet comment. Their son, Phil, who has three sons of his own, once told his parents: "I love that you love our children."

Phil's words are perhaps the key to building strong bonds with our grandchildren. The two most important things we can do as parents and grandparents are to love each other and to let our children and grandchildren know that we love them.

Deep down, I think Steve and I want to be good grandparents because we want them to remember us and perhaps share stories of our adventures with *their* children and great-grandchildren, some of whom we may never meet.

And, just between you and me, that's also the main reason we're writing this book. Now if we can just get them to put the devices away long enough to read it! (Maybe the e-book?)

When all the grandkids aren't outside playing sand volleyball or their made-up "Jason Bourne" game, they're usually squeezing around a coffee table to play a board game.

48
We Are Family

In June of 1996, Mary and I got together with friends Millie, John, Margo, and Tom to plan our annual summer mini-vacation.

Margo brought with her a travel magazine and read to us about "descending into the Root River Valley of Southeast Minnesota where time slows down, and relaxation begins as you ride an inflated tube three hours on the lazy river."

The adjectives "slow, relaxed, and lazy" got our attention. We were teachers and administrators, and we were looking forward to summer vacation. We began to plan three glorious days together to unwind and enjoy a small part of our summer.

That was the first of many trips to the Root River and the Southeast Minnesota towns of Lanesboro and Whalan for Mary and me. There are campgrounds in the valley, nice rail trails for walking or biking, and tubing or kayaking on the river. There's also an abundance of wildlife—I saw a bald eagle in the wild for the first time ever along the river.

The Root River runs in a deep valley surrounded by 300-foot limestone bluffs untouched by ancient glaciers. A century ago, a railroad was built alongside the river heading westward. It winds its way next to the river from Houston through Whalan and Lanesboro to Fountain at the top of the bluffs. The railroad was eventually turned into a perfect paved hiking and biking trail.

Mary and I celebrated our 29th wedding anniversary on May 29, 2000, at a countryside bed-and-breakfast near Lanesboro, mostly because we had enjoyed our first trip to the Root River area with our friends. Starting in town by the Visitor's Center, we rode the trail to Whalan on a busy Memorial Day weekend.

As we biked through the small village, a road branched to the left and up a small hill. We were curious about where the road led, so we followed it. We didn't know it then, but that ride up the hill was the beginning of a family tradition lasting 23 years and counting.

At the top of the slope, we saw a man on a ladder absorbed in the task of attaching log cabin siding to a building. We stopped to chat with him and found out his name was Larry, the owner of Cedar Valley Resort which would be opening the next year. Larry and his wife Sheryl were converting his family's old mink farm refrigerator building into two three-bedroom cabins.

Larry was so friendly and enthusiastic about his plans for the resort that Mary and I were caught up in the excitement too. We asked about costs and reservations for the next year.

With the birth of our first grandchildren early in 2000, we had begun discussing how we could keep our family close as our numbers increased, which now included our three children, their spouses, two grandsons, and, as it turned out, eight more grandchildren yet to be born.

Cedar Valley Resort would be the perfect destination for our small but growing family, and we could all stay in one cabin, relaxing and catching up on each other's lives. We decided that the CVR vacation would be a gift to our kids to honor and celebrate their wedding anniversaries.

The bonus was it would give the grandchildren, who live in different parts of the state, extended time to play together and strengthen the bonds of family that Mary and I visualized for us all. We hoped they would be close friends as well as cousins.

The trips to Cedar Valley Resort have been a time of fun activities with lots of miles put on our bikes, tubing, roasting marshmallows as we sat around the fire, and many memories made together as a family. Ensuring that the tradition continues requires intentional effort to "take time to make time; make time to be there..." as recommended by the Little River Band.

The biggest challenge is finding dates that will work for everyone, which involves matching up at least four different family calendars, reflecting 19 different schedules, to find four days each year when no one has other commitments. It's not quite as difficult as climbing Mt. Everest, but I think you get what I mean. Even so, the Cedar Valley Resort trips have been an important experience for us each year, serving as a refreshing reminder of who we are as a family.

One of my favorite memories is the time when Larry gave Jack and Tim, our two oldest grandsons, a ride on his John Deere Gator around the property. We're glad that we thought to capture the delight that was obvious on their faces in the photos.

Tubing is always a big part of every trip. We rented big yellow tubes from CVR and went floating down the river under the bridge at Whalan. When there were babies and toddlers too young to tube, Mary and I stayed at the cabin with them, but we always went to the bridge to see the parents and older children float by and to take lots of pictures.

Mary and I have so many happy memories of our Cedar Valley Resort vacations, but we thought it'd be interesting to ask the grandkids what their favorite memories are.

Allison, now 21 and in baking school, remembers going tubing one year when she and her cousin Anna were too young to be in tubes alone. Their parents put them together in a small raft we sometimes used to carry cold beverages while rafting.

"We got really hot," Ally said, "so to cool off, we took the bucket hats on our heads and dunked them in the water. Then we wrung them out in the raft, making our own little swimming pool while floating down the river."

Charlie, 20, a USD student studying theatre performance and stage construction, said the very competitive volleyball games he and his cousins played while the adults watched from the cabin's front deck were some of his favorite memories.

"I also remember waiting on the first day for everyone to arrive, and as soon as we had two families, the sand volleyball would begin," he said, adding, "One year, the game lasted far into the evening, eventually stopping when the sun went down. I believe a masculine game of sand volleyball was repeated several times. Super committed, I was finding sand on me for days!"

We couldn't believe the kids' determination to finish a game until the last rays of sunlight left the sky. Even then, they probably quit mostly because it was time to make s'mores.

Tim, 23, a vocal music major, has so many memories that he said it was "super difficult to pick just one favorite story or experience. I have plenty of fond memories of tubing/biking, but also lots of great memories of just hanging out in the cabins with the cousins playing Slime, the triennial game of Munchkin, and watching the British TV show, *Hunted*."

Another of Tim's favorites was "the first time the older cousins all biked to Lanesboro (without the parents)," he said. "I remember it really fondly. We just hung out, grabbed ice cream, looked through all of the overpriced touristy shops, and I remember it being such a blast! I definitely think the trips brought us closer as a family. I look forward to spending time with you guys (Grandma and Grandpa) and all of the extended family every year!"

There were two years when we vacationed in other locations, but we returned to Cedar Valley Resort. Tim said he enjoyed those trips, too, summarizing our time together like this: "I'd say it has less to do with where we are and more to do with the fact that we're together as a family! I love you guys…"

Okay, I'll admit it. Tim's last two lines choked me up and brought tears to my eyes.

Our youngest grandson, Caleb, a sophomore in high school, said, "Getting ice cream every time we biked to Lanesboro was fun. Stopping for a fallen tree and going under it with our bikes was pretty good too."

Since one purpose of the trip was to celebrate our children's wedding anniversaries, we set aside a night for an anniversary dinner. The grandchildren made and served a special meal for their parents. When the kids were old enough to stay alone, all the adults went to a restaurant for dinner, leaving them at home with pizzas. Our oldest grandson Jack remembers those nights as his best memories.

"My favorite part of every vacation at Cedar Valley is the evening that all the parents go out to eat for dinner, leaving us kids at the cabin with a pizza and unlimited TV for a couple of hours. We're all basically adults now and can fend for ourselves, so the novelty has worn off a bit (I think), but it was always exciting to me when the adults left, and we were free to do whatever we wanted."

Sam, who studied business at University of Northern Iowa, said, "One of my favorite memories is from this last year, going to the baseball field and playing a couple of pick-up baseball games. Despite a lack of players and equipment, we still had some pretty competitive games. Along with a bunch of other games we've played at the cabins, the cousins are really good at entertaining ourselves with (mostly) friendly competition."

Anna, an elementary ed major at Indiana Wesleyan University, said she liked baseball and sand volleyball competitions adding, "And Jason Bourne, of course." To the best of our knowledge, "Jason Bourne" is a game the grandkids made up based on the spy thriller movie character. It always has to be dark when they start playing. Beyond that, we adults know nothing about this special game except that the grandkids would play for hours.

Rowan, a senior in high school, agreed: "Jason Bourne has definitely been one of my favorite activities at Cedar Valley. I have a ton of good memories of running around the whole resort trying not to get caught by any of the cousins. For sure, some of my best memories happened there."

The first year we vacationed at Cedar Valley Resort, we stayed in a four-bedroom cabin, and our two six-month-old grandsons slept in their parents' rooms. As our family expanded, and the kids didn't need to sleep in their parents' rooms anymore, we moved up to a six-bedroom cabin that has been our favorite for many years.

But with the grandkids growing into young adults and adding granddaughter-in-law Makayla last year, there is a need for more space. For next summer, we have reserved an eight-bedroom, six-bathroom cabin with both upstairs and downstairs family rooms, which should give us plenty of elbow room.

After daughter Laura takes the traditional family picture on our last morning, it is with a bittersweet feeling that we climb back into our loaded vehicles and begin the drive up out of the valley.

But we leave knowing the family bond that ties us together grows stronger, ensuring a solid and trusted unit. We hope our children and grandchildren realize how much we love them, just as we hope their love for each other stays forever in their hearts.

Because we are family.

The Steele family at Cedar Valley Resort, minus Charlie, who couldn't be with us this year due to a summer internship. In his absence, we had a bigger-than-life-sized picture of him made so he could be in all the family photos.

49
I Guess That's Why They Call It the Blues

A year ago, I decided our front door should be blue. Everything else about the exterior of our house is beigy-grey, or according to the label on the paint can, Dove Grey. Even the inside walls are beigy-grey, and we have grey furniture in our main sitting room. I like it that way, but I decided our door should be blue for unknown reasons.

Steve was reluctant to paint—he'd done a lot of painting in the summers when our kids were young to make a little extra cash. But he was a good sport about it. As usual, when we tackle a painting project, he paints all of the time-consuming trim, which takes patience and attention to detail, and I paint the wide-open spaces because I paint quickly and need to see progress NOW. (That pretty much sums up our personalities, too, now that I think about it.) I figured we'd finish the job in an hour or two.

Instead, it took almost an hour to pick out the paint, examining and comparing all the paint swatches to choose just the right blue-grey color I was hoping for. After brushing a couple of swipes onto the door, I immediately realized it was way too blue—more of a dark royal blue than a blue-grey.

Fortunately, we had a leftover bucket of Dove Grey paint in a garage cupboard, so I mixed the too-bright blue with the too-conservative beigey-grey until I was satisfied with the result. (In the can, anyway.) By the time we started painting again with the newly mixed blue-grey, another hour had passed.

The first coat didn't cover the beige-grey well, so we had to give it another coat. And another. And another. Finally, after five coats, we called it done (by then, five hours had passed).

But the door still wasn't the blue-grey I had pictured in my mind. Whenever we turned into the driveway, I would look at the in-your-face too-blue door and cringe.

Fast forward a year. I knew I wanted to re-mix the two colors and try again. I also knew that Steve would think mixing paint and starting the process over was ridiculous and unnecessary. Plus, he had the hardest part of the job—the trim.

So, I devised a plan. On a nice day, I said to my husband of almost 52 years, "I have a proposition for you." His ears perked up at that comment. "If you'll paint the trim on the front door, I'll do the wide-open spaces, AND I'll take you to the movie, "Guardians of the Galaxy."

We rarely go to movies (I prefer to watch them at home so we can pause for bathroom and popcorn breaks), and we never go to shoot-'em-up, excessively violent shows glorifying brutality. (My choice—Steve rather likes some of them.) I was sure it would be difficult for him to turn me down.

I Guess That's Why They Call It the Blues

After giving it a couple of minutes thought, Steve took the deal. I added more blue paint to the remaining Dove Grey paint from last year and started my part of the job.

(A sidenote: While sitting on a 5-gallon bucket turned upside down so I could reach the bottom of the door, my cell phone, handed down to me by my granddaughter, Anna, slipped out of my pocket and into the bucket of blue paint. With cat-like reflexes, I pulled the phone out of the paint bucket before it sunk to the bottom, but it never worked the same after that… I now have a new phone.)

I painted for about two hours (that includes the time spent cleaning the paint from my phone), and then Steve worked another couple of hours finishing the trim and cleaning up afterward.

The result? Good news and bad news. The good news is that it only took one coat this time. The bad news? It *still* isn't quite the blue-grey I was hoping for. Sigh. Maybe I should have added more of a grey-based paint instead of beige to the blue. I decided to give it some time and see if it would grow on me.

In the meantime, I kept my end of the deal. We went to "Guardians of the Galaxy" on senior night (actually, a 5 p.m. start, which is plenty late for us seniors).

Let's just say that I now know why people carry Glocks and AR-15s into neighborhoods, schools, businesses, and shopping malls and then shoot everyone in sight. I'm guessing 75% of the movie included scenes with actors shooting, exploding, or otherwise killing characters. Most weren't actually human—they were weird, freaky animals/space aliens/monster-type beings.

Many of these ultra-violent movies, including "Guardians,"

are also video games wildly popular among young people. So, when they're not watching violence on the big screen, they're watching *and participating in* the savagery on their devices.

And if that wasn't enough to give it two thumbs down, it lasted 150 minutes! Two and one-half hours of almost nothing but mayhem, destruction, and executions. It was so loud I thought my ears might fall off.

Mary's review of "Guardians of the Galaxy"

As we walked out the door, I asked Steve what he thought about the movie (before I blurted out my opinion of the show like I usually do.) He replied, "It may have been the worst movie I've ever seen!" I was surprised and pleased. No,

I Guess That's Why They Call It the Blues

I was *relieved* that he felt the same way I did.

As for the still-not-the-right-color-blue door... Maybe another coat next year?

The infamous blue door

50
A Change Would Do You Good

A man from the backcountry and his son were visiting a big city for the first time. They looked around in awe at the bright lights, tall buildings, and bustling streets. Then they walked into the lobby of a fancy hotel and sat down on the plush chairs facing the elevator, not knowing what the newfangled contraption was.

The two hadn't been sitting long before they saw a wrinkled, sour-faced woman enter the elevator. The doors closed. A few minutes later, the doors opened, and a beautiful young woman walked out, flashing them a dazzling smile.

In amazement, the man looked at his son and said, "Boy, go get your ma!"

If changing other people and ourselves was that easy, life would be a breeze, wouldn't it? Unfortunately, humans aren't transformed by simply walking into a metal box and closing the door.

Change is difficult. Why is that? I went to my friend Google, and this is how Artificial Intelligence (AI) answered my question:

It can be hard to change oneself or others for many reasons. Some of these reasons include fear of the unknown, lack of motivation, lack of purpose and self-control, impatience, worrying about what other people think, and fear of failure. Change can also be difficult because it can challenge how we think, how we work, the quality of our relationships, and even our physical security or sense of identity.

Change can be especially challenging for married couples. However, it's not always bad to encourage your partner to change. First Corinthians 13 says that husbands and wives should always expect the best of each other and help them reach their full potential.

I read a story about Pete Flaherty, mayor of Pittsburgh in the 1970s. He and his wife, Nancy, were standing on a sidewalk surveying a city construction project when one of the laborers working at the site called out to them.

"Hey, Nancy, remember me? We used to date when we were in high school!"

Later, Mayor Pete teased his wife about the incident. "Aren't you glad you married me? Just think, if you had married your old boyfriend, you would be the wife of a construction worker."

Nancy looked her husband in the eye and said firmly, "No, if I had married him, **he** would be mayor of Pittsburgh!"

She was certainly confident about changing her could-have-been spouse! However, trying to change your partner may negatively affect the relationship.

It's important I clarify that when I talk about trying to change your mate, I'm not referring to destructive traits that can ruin relationships to the point of no return: aggression, bullying, physical or emotional abuse, withholding affection, addictions, including alcohol, drugs, and gambling. Those traits may be impossible to change unless a person wants to change, and even so, they will likely require professional counseling.

Instead, I'm talking about the less consequential but annoying things like not putting things back where they belong, nagging, not putting the toilet seat down, not listening, procrastinating, spending too much money... I'm sure you could add to this list.

You've probably heard of the book, *Men Are from Mars, Women Are from Venus*, published in the '70s. It points out the psychological and emotional differences between men and women. Sometimes the solution is to accept that the two of you aren't exactly alike and to learn to live with the differences—and perhaps even celebrate them.

Maya Angelou said, "If you don't like something, change it. If you can't change it, change your attitude." She may have been referring to the world's problems, but I think it also applies to relationships. It's sometimes more effective to change ourselves since we have more control over ourselves than others.

Steve and I have been learning lessons about changing each other and ourselves throughout our marriage. (We both get annoyed over silly things like the correct way to load a dishwasher.) But the things we can't change are the most difficult to deal with.

A Change Would Do You Good

Over the last several years, Steve's hearing loss has become a challenging issue for both of us. I feel like I repeat nearly everything I say to him because he doesn't hear me the first (or second or third) time.

I sometimes wonder, "Is he not hearing me, not understanding, or not listening?" I struggle with trying not to take it personally.

As frustrating as it is for me, his hearing loss has to be much more so for him. In large groups or when there's a lot of noise around him, like at a busy restaurant, I know he doesn't hear all of the conversations at our table. I can tell he is faking it. He nods his head at appropriate times, but he tells me later that he didn't hear or understand some or most of the discussion.

We both recognize that his hearing impairment is a long-term problem we'll have to continue dealing with, and it will likely worsen. Steve has seen two excellent audiologists and has possibly the best hearing aids available for his particular impairment. He also wears a small microphone attached to his shirt to pick up voices. And still, his hearing loss is significant.

A potential "cure" might be cochlear implants. I'm all for them, not having researched much, but Steve is less enthusiastic. He watched a YouTube video on the procedure, which added to his hesitancy to pursue the possibility because it mentioned that the implants could result in losing his remaining natural hearing. (Rarely, but still, something to consider.) Steve recently talked to a man who had good results from cochlear implants and afterward made an appointment to consult with a specialist later this year.

Like Steve, I have my impairments. My hearing isn't great either, but a bigger concern is that my memory is failing. I sometimes share misinformation with Steve and others because I've forgotten the correct dates, numbers, conversations, names of people I should know, or where I put things.

I frequently ask Steve questions like: *Did we see that movie?* If he says we have, my next question is: *Did we like it?*

A couple of times a week, I tell Steve that I've put down my phone and I don't know where it is. I have to ask him to call my phone so I can locate it. I also frequently lose my car keys, laptop mouse, and TV remote. I know that I could improve my memory by focusing on one thought or conversation at a time instead of being distracted by bright, shiny objects.

> It was a sad and disappointing day when I discovered my universal remote control did not, in fact, control the universe.
> (Not even remotely.)

And it's not just the memory issue I'm concerned about. For example, I usually use the same chair to work on my laptop and watch TV, and I almost always have my phone with me. Occasionally, I have pointed my phone or mouse toward the TV to change the channel. (BTW, it doesn't work. But don't tell Steve that I've confused the devices, or he'll start looking for a "nice home" for me.)

I don't know how to improve my memory other than focusing more. There are dozens of products advertised on TV that supposedly make you sharper, but I'm too skeptical to try them.

Ultimately, we will just have to accept that there are some things we can't change about each other or ourselves, and it will take communication, understanding, empathy, resilience, and patience to get through our golden years.

Paraphrasing the familiar words of St. Francis of Assisi:

We need to ask God to give us the courage to change the things we can change, the serenity to accept the things we cannot, and the wisdom to know the difference.

Not as eloquent but equally applicable is this meme about dealing with our differences:

"Men are from Earth. Women are from Earth. Get over it!"

51

These Are the Best Days of Our Lives

The title for this episode was inspired by Bryan Adams's song, "Summer of '69." The song has special meaning for us because Mary and I both graduated from high school in 1969.

However, we took some liberties with the original line in the song that says, "Those were the best days of our lives."

That lyric implies that life will never be as good as it was 50-some years ago, and we would challenge that claim. We prefer to think that those who have a positive attitude about growing older, and are willing to leave things in the past that hold them back but still remember the valuable lessons they learned along the way, are more likely to find that the best days of their lives are yet to come.

But it's sometimes difficult to determine what is worth hanging on to and what we should let go.

These Are the Best Days of Our Lives

The 1981 movie, "Cannonball Run," is about an outlaw cross-country car race. One of our favorite scenes is just before the start of the race when the Italian driver rips off the rearview mirror and explains to his stunned driving partner, "What-sa behind-a me, it's-a not important!"

Leaving behind the baggage that weighs us down will help us to have a more fulfilling future. However, there are things from our past that are best forgotten. I asked Mary what material things she'd leave behind as she looks to the future.

"I loved some of the fashions when I was in high school: bell-bottom jeans, shifts (straight dresses), miniskirts, go-go boots, psychedelic colors, and anything with a hippie look," she says, adding, "but some of those fads look pretty silly to me now. I think it's best to leave most of them back in the '60s where they belong."

Unlike Mary, I didn't think much about fashion growing up. My wardrobe was mostly hand-me-downs from my brothers—and they were, by no means, "clothes horses." The rest of my small wardrobe consisted of a mix of store-bought clothes and purchases from the thrift store in town.

Another popular style in the '70s was the wide, paisley ties. How did we tie those things without ending up with a knot the size of our heads? Those fads didn't last long, and I'm happy to leave them in the past.

Mary said another thing she'd leave behind is "stuff."

"We're not hoarders. We try to buy only items that we need and are functional. That excludes knick-knacks or doo-dads serving no purpose but to collect dust. I try to practice 'catch and release' when I shop," Mary says. "I see something I like, pick it up, think about it for a minute, and ask myself, 'Do I need it? Does it have a function? Am I just buying it to replace a similar item I already have, but I'm tired of the color or design? If I answer no, no, and yes, then I let it go. That's the theory, anyway. However, I admit I'm better at catching than releasing."

I like Mary's catch-and-release strategy, and I support her in that. I know that for her, a clearance tag is like a shiny spoon in front of a small-mouth bass. (I also admit to loving clearance sales almost as much as Mary.)

Decluttering is on our To-Do-Soon List, as is making several trips to our local second-hand store, Many Hands Market, which benefits missions in Haiti. Two of our good friends are missionaries in Haiti.

I must confess that there are some things I am more reluctant to give away than Mary. For example, I have difficulty letting go of ragged but soft sweatshirts and comfortable but well-worn shoes. Those items of clothing and I have been through a lot together, and although the shirts might have some holes and the shoes are scuffed, it's like getting rid of old friends.

"If we don't sort through and give away our 'stuff' now," Mary says, "I'm afraid that when we're gone, our kids will back up a big dump truck to our front door, fill it up, and take it to the landfill. They may have just thrown away valuable items like birth certificates, baby pictures, priceless heirlooms like their preschool art projects, and cans of food that haven't reached their freshness dates. (Or that may be a little past. Have I taught them *nothing*?)."

Besides the tangible things we want to leave behind, there are intangible things like attitudes, emotions, and even some memories that are best left in the past. Doing so can help move us toward success and growth.

Mary says there are several intangible things she wants to

leave behind, including "guilt, holding grudges, and anxieties. Those are much harder to give up than the physical things we've accumulated."

I'm guessing I'm not the only adult in their '70s who still questions whether they are capable and worthy of being listened to or have thoughts that should be heard. It's an internal battle of anxious self-doubt, and I would leave it behind in a heartbeat.

As to what tangible things we'd take into the future, many are the same as we listed in our chapter titled "Our Favorite Things," with the top item being photo albums filled with pictures of our kids and grandchildren, trips and vacations, and friends—all precious because they remind us of those we love and who love us.

Precious things we'll take into the future: Memories of sitting around a campfire, roasting marshmallows, chatting, and laughing with our children and grandchildren.

We both had happy but not fairytale childhoods, and we agree that among the intangible things we'd take into the future are those early memories that will continue to give us joy.

Mary says she'd also want to take music from the past 60 years with her into the coming decades.

"Growing up, we didn't have many records in our house. But late at night, when the radio reception was best, I'd listen to WLS in Chicago playing the hits. I still enjoy a variety of music from my teen years, but I also appreciate many of today's popular singers," she says. "My list of favorites is too long to list here, but they stretch from Elvis Presley and the Beatles to Bob Dylan and Otis Redding to Lady Gaga and Lewis Capaldi. And I love songs from my favorite Broadway musicals."

While writing this book, I discovered that the past is a pleasant place for me. I enjoy the small successes I've experienced, and I have found that there are instructive moments from 60 years ago that are still guiding principles for me today. But some of those lessons learned in the past are tied to bad experiences that you might think I'd want to forget.

Here's an example of the complexity of determining what to let go of and what to hang on to. My friends in elementary school called me "Hambone." Some kids who weren't my friends called me "Fatso."

There came a day in junior high when I made a commitment to myself: "I will never be fat again." I started doing running workouts and lifting weights to get in shape. I wanted to be good at football like my brothers.

Being overweight and being dubbed "fatso" are memories

some would choose to leave behind, but I can't. I promised myself I'd get fit, and, for better or for worse, remembering the name-calling helps me keep that promise.

It's never too late to finally let go of things that weigh us down or to start carrying forward those things from our past that strengthen and motivate us to help make today and the days that follow the best days of our lives.

As Eleanor Roosevelt eloquently said, "Today is the oldest you have ever been and the youngest you will ever be again."

Start now. Today.

Epilogue: Put a Little Love in Your Heart

You may have noticed that we are very quick to offer advice (or, at least, one of us is). The word *advice* has a negative connotation, so instead, let's call our attempts at wisdom *encouragement* or *suggestions,* shall we?

Suggestion #1: As we come to the end of our memoir, and at the risk of sounding like a broken record, we want to encourage every reader, regardless of age, to keep a journal. We think it's important that everyone record their stories for their children and their children's children and beyond. That doesn't mean you have to publish a book like we have chosen to do. Just write down (or record on video or audiotape) your memories, thoughts, a little genealogy, and anything else you want future generations to know about you.

It's not difficult to do, and there is plenty of help to guide you through the process. Libraries, art centers, senior centers, and community colleges sometimes offer classes on "Writing Your Story." There is also information online or in your library about how to write a memoir.

Or check out a product like Storyworth, which helps you create a photo journal by suggesting writing prompts. You write chapters, submit photos, and then Storyworth publishes your book just for you. A great gift idea for parents or grandparents!

Steve's sister-in-law, Helen Steele, found journals his mom

had written between 1980 and 1995. Doris was 60 when she started writing in them and continued through age 75. She wrote her thoughts in spiral notebooks—showing that you don't need a fancy cloth-covered journal to start writing.

Here is one of the many stories that Doris recorded in her notebooks. This one tells of a "basket social" in 1925 to raise funds for playground equipment for her rural school:

"Every lady and every girl made a decorated lunch box filled with goodies, and the husbands and boyfriends bid on them. Mother made one for me, a shoebox covered with pink crepe paper with white ruffling. Very pretty. A romantic young swain bid $2.50 (a huge amount!), thinking it belonged to his

Epilogue: Put a Little Love in Your Heart

girlfriend. Can you imagine his chagrin when he found it belonged to a 5-year-old? And we had to eat lunch together!"

Although the journals don't include photos, Helen collected all the Doris and Silas Steele family photos she could find and spent countless hours assembling them into two very large photo books for Doris's 90th birthday.

Doris is proof that you can start writing at any age, on any scraps of paper you might have lying around the house, and write about ordinary events that will be of interest to future generations.

Suggestion #2: Commit to making this a better world by being kind to each other, loving everyone, and sharing our blessings with those who need it most. Sometimes, especially when we watch the evening news, we shake our heads, wring our hands, and wonder what will become of us. Often, we feel sad, afraid, helpless, and hopeless.

But we all can, and should, play a part in improving our world. We can't sit idly by and hope things improve—we must **do** something.

Nelson Mandela said that no one is born hating another person because of their color, religion, or background. People learn to hate, and if they can learn to hate, they can be taught to love. Once we learn to love, we must teach our children to love.

How? First, by ensuring that our children—and others—see love, graciousness, and compassion in us. Start small: smile, speak with kindness, show genuine interest in others, be encouraging. Move on to bigger steps: volunteer, donate to worthy causes, do what you can to preserve the environment, and learn about other cultures and religions. To change the world, we must first change ourselves.

TIMES THEY ARE A-CHANGIN'

We hope we've motivated you to share your story with others and to make a difference one step at a time. We also hope you've enjoyed these blasts from the past and that our words, memes, art prints, photos, and song lyrics have brought back many happy memories for you.

Art Print by Gabriel Andreas, courtesy of StoryPeople, Decorah, IA.

We Get by With a Little Help From Our Friends

There are several people we want to recognize for their contributions to this book:

The bride and groom cartoon figures at the beginning of each chapter to indicate which one of us wrote it were illustrated by our creative granddaughter, **Anna Eckert**. Thanks, Anna!

Nick LaPointe loaned us the beautiful typewriter used on the cover photo. It doesn't just sit around collecting dust—he uses it to compose song lyrics. We're so impressed! Using computers for word processing has spoiled most of us.

Helen Steele uncovered Doris's journals from 30+ years ago, which are a treasure to the Steele family. She also completed a task many of us only think about—putting all the family photos into two huge photo albums. Priceless!

A big thank you to the folks at **StoryPeople** who allowed us to use their fantastically creative art and wisdom. They said in a few words what it took us a whole chapter to say. A special "hats off" to Ellen, whom I bombarded with emails and requests. She patiently replied to every single one of my frantic messages. Shop for StoryPeople's many other prints, ornaments, and a large variety of gift items at local book and gift stores or at **storypeople.com**.

Laura Steele Eckert photographed and designed the cover and did all of the formatting of the book for publishing. After we sent *Betty: A Memoir* off to Amazon for publishing, she swore she'd never do another book. But, enough time passed that she'd forgotten some of the pain, and we were able to convince her it was worth doing again. You can see Laura's photography work at **newcreationphotography.com**.

Authors' Notes: Looks Like We Made It

All good things must end someday, according to Chad & Jeremy's "A Summer Song." That applies to our story, Times They Are A-Changin': As Told by a Couple Happily Married (Most Days) for 50+ Years.

We are writing this analysis together after alternating authorship for the previous 51 episodes for Amazon's platform, Kindle Vella. It's a bittersweet and almost surreal experience to now turn it into a book. A year ago, I don't think either of us would have believed we could write a book together, much less write it in 5 months and then totally revise and publish it with photos in a year.

Although it's been fun, and we've learned a lot writing together, churning out two episodes (as they refer to "chapters" on Kindle Vella) a week was sometimes stressful. It seems like no matter how early in the week we started writing, we were usually putting on the final touches late into the night. Since we've both been retired for several years, we are used to doing what we want when we want.

Before we began writing these final thoughts, we looked back at the introduction to our story to see if the finished project was what we anticipated it would be. In the intro, we said we'd write in a "he-said, she-said" format, covering topics ranging from family life to current events over the past 70 years. We also said, "We'll see how the world, the country, and our lives have changed over the past seven decades. Or not."

To wrap up this project, we asked ourselves these questions:

Did we accomplish our objectives?

Mary: We didn't use the "he-said, she-said" strategy like we'd planned. Instead of writing alternate chapters on the same topics showing our differing views, we chose our own themes each week. That may be because we think alike on many topics, which wouldn't make for exciting reading. However, we use a he-said, she-said format for this "Authors' Notes" section to avoid all those quotation marks...

Steve: We accomplished what we set out to do. We wanted to introduce ourselves to our family and the rest of the world. We wanted to show how things have changed in our lives, and I think we accomplished both objectives.

One reason why we met that goal is *because* we didn't both write about the same topics. Instead, we were able to share a broader range of ideas and opinions by writing about each of our own personal experiences and viewpoints about life, culture, and technology over the last 70 years.

"He said, she said" can be entertaining and enlightening if each writer has more varied experiences and opinions. Mary and I think alike on a wide range of topics. Who wants to read chapters consisting of two words: "Me Too?" In a sense, the narrative form we used allowed us some room to roam and share topics about us as individuals that are important to us.

What have we learned from writing our story?

Steve: I enjoy research but struggled to bring the pieces together. Mary has an amazing gift (I think it comes from her quilt-making experience) of collecting information, choosing only the most relevant pieces, and stitching them all together coherently.

We have different writing styles and outcomes. Since I am a retired teacher and have served church groups as a pastor and leader, I tend to write more seriously, trying to teach some important lessons in each chapter.

Mary: Steve's comments about our writing styles is on the nose. I write like a journalist, and he writes like a pastor turned teacher.

Another difference: Steve tends to give lots of background upfront and eventually gets around to clarifying his theme and finally making his point. Sometimes, when proofreading his work, I get lost in the tangle of background information and wonder where he's going with it. Journalists call that "burying the lede."

When I write, I get to the point quickly. I tell *who, what, when, where, how, and sometimes why* at the top of the story. That's how all good newspaper stories are written. Then reporters fill in with other interesting but less critical information. (*Just the facts, ma'am.*)

However, that is *not* the best way to write a memoir.

When my kids proofread my first draft of *Betty: A Memoir*, they said it "sounded like a newspaper reporter wrote it." That's when I realized it was okay to include more than just the core facts when writing a memoir.

When people pick up a newspaper, they want to read only articles of interest to them and to read them quickly. You may have noticed that some online news articles start by printing at the top how long it will take to read the story.

TIMES THEY ARE A-CHANGIN'

Readers who pick up a book know they're in it for the long haul. I am currently reading *Covenant of Water*, which is 724 pages long. But the author, Abraham Verghese, is such an excellent writer that I don't mind that the book is three inches thick, except that it will take me a while to get to the next book on my To-Read stack.

When it comes to writing a memoir, I realized I could and should share my thoughts, feelings, and opinions—all things that aren't appropriate in news stories. Many readers of "Betty" said that they felt I was in the room talking to them when they were reading the book, a comment I loved to hear. But using that personal voice wouldn't be allowed when writing news stories.

What have we learned about ourselves?

Steve: I found I have feelings that I still need to work through—some about family relationships, others about religious issues and their power to lead or mislead, depending on how truth is understood.

Mary: I've learned that I enjoy writing and reading memoirs. I've been asked if I'd ever consider writing fiction, but I don't think I have the creative mind and imagination it takes to write novels. My forte is arranging facts into a (hopefully) readable and interesting story.

How are we alike?

Steve: Mary and I agree on the most critical topics, including child raising, the importance of families, ethics, religion, faith, grace, politics, and the direction of our lives.

Mary: I agree that we agree...

How are we different?

Steve: I am a teacher and talker, though not especially outgoing. I want to tell listeners what they should do or how and why they should change their lives.

Mary is an organizer and doer who likes to get things done. When I see someone in need, I think about sharing some money. Mary doesn't think about it—she does what needs to be done. Simple as that.

Mary: I am a spontaneous planner. (Is that an oxymoron?) I do like to plan, organize, and even color code, but I am also more apt to make snap decisions than Steve or do something on the spur of the moment. He prefers to think and ponder before making a move. He loves puzzles and would be a good chess player. Both take too much patience for me. I'd be better at ping-pong than puzzles.

How have we grown, and what changes have we seen because of this project?

Mary: Although we cook, clean, socialize, and travel together, this is the first time we've actually *worked* together. (We don't do enough cooking and cleaning to call those things "work.") Overall, it's been a good experience, and I think we understand each other better and are closer because of it.

Steve: It has been humbling for me. Writing the book forced me to think about the truth and accuracy of everything I wrote. Every written word, including family stories, the trips we've taken, and the jobs we've held, has to be told with as much accuracy as my memories can provide.

Also, I've discovered I don't like to be criticized or to be a critic. Good writing requires honest feedback. Mary is good at accepting *and* giving it. I don't do either as well as I should.

What has surprised us about co-authoring a book?

TIMES THEY ARE A-CHANGIN'

Mary: I am surprised at how many hours we've spent writing, proofreading, editing, revising, and publishing these chapters. We also posted Facebook previews to promote each new episode published on Kindle Vella. I could zip right through the posts, but most chapters took me several hours, and a few took several days. Steve has clocked as many hours as I have and maybe more.

Steve: Definitely the deadlines. It's not something you do once to get done and hand in (like some of my middle school homework assignments). But if it weren't for the Kindle Vella weekly deadlines, I would only be about half done, if that.

Mary tells me that writing is a process that, in some ways, is like forming a clay sculpture. You take a block of clay and make it into a work of art, but it takes time and patience. You add some clay here, and you take some out there. I've discovered that good writing involves shaping and smoothing, often rewriting and searching for a more understandable or articulate way to express your thoughts. Sometimes, after hours of work, you have to start over with your lump of clay. But the end product gives me a sense of accomplishment.

Is it true that couples who have been together a long time begin to look alike? Think alike?

Mary: To be honest, we've been together so long that I can't remember if we were alike when we started out together or if we grew to be more alike as the decades flew by. Probably some of both. We often finish each other's sentences and seem to have invented our own sign language.

Steve: We're not psychic, but we know each other well enough that sometimes we can read each other's minds. I often think, "Mary will like..." Or, "Mary's thinking about..."

Regarding looking alike, I have to chuckle because I've thought that some people must wonder if we are related. Our hair color and complexions are similar—reddish hair and pale European stock from the British Isles.

Why stop at 51 chapters?

Mary and Steve: The title says our story will be "a look back at the past seven decades," so when we had shared experiences and events from each of those decades, we knew it was time to wind it down.

Choosing the exact number was somewhat arbitrary, but it seemed right to us because '51 was the year we were born, and it's also the number of years we'd been married when the writing was finished for Kindle Vella.

What are we looking forward to in the next couple of decades? What aren't we looking forward to?

Steve: We have friends and family to visit and to travel with for as long as we're able. I am not a fan of the physical and mental toll that aging takes on us all. But we'll "keep on going so we can keep on going." Our faith will take us the rest of the way.

Mary: We were going to use the title "All Good Things Must End Some Day" for this last entry. We even discussed expanding the theme to write not only about the book's ending, but also to our "ending."

We decided after some discussion that it would be too much of a downer. We laughed a lot about topics we might have included in that chapter that won't be written. We even came up with the perfect title: "Knock, Knock, Knocking on Heaven's Door."

What happens next?

TIMES THEY ARE A-CHANGIN'

Mary: We'll start editing, revising, and collecting photos. Our daughter, Laura Eckert, will format the book, edit all photos, and design the cover, as she did for *Betty: A Memoir*. Then we'll submit it to Amazon/Kindle for publication into hardcover, paperback, and e-book formats, hopefully in time for Christmas.

Steve: I'll be helping with all of the above. Tracking down photos will be a big task, but pictures will bring the book together and be an advantage over the Kindle Vella format, which doesn't allow images.

What comes next? Will we write another book?

Mary: I will stay busy doing everything we've put off while writing *Times*. We'll be leading some Memoir Writing Workshops and doing book signings and readings—events we've put on hold.

However, I'm thinking about writing a story I think should be told. I'm pondering the question: Do I have the desire and stamina to tell it? More about that on my Facebook business page down the road. To access the page, follow me at Mary McSwain Steele – Author.

Steve: We're considering doing an audio version of "Betty." And, in our wildest dreams, what about a screenplay?

Mary: LOL. I'd love for "Betty" to be made into a movie, but I think there's little chance of that happening. Just in case, I've thought about actors I'd like to see play my mom (Meryl Streep), younger me (Julia Roberts with reddish blonde hair—a stretch, for sure, but I *like* her), and older me (Jane Fonda).

One last thought about writing another book—it's a little like childbirth. An undefined length of time must pass before we forget the pain and only remember the joy of bringing a baby (or a book) into this world. (P.S. My apologies to all the

Looks Like We Made It

moms reading this for comparing writing to labor and likening our book to your babies!)

Steve and Mary watch the sun set on the beach.
(Photo by Lori Adams)

Also by Mary McSwain Steele

Betty: A Memoir

"Betty" is a beautiful story of a single mother's courage in life and death. Her stunning deathbed confession and final request leave her daughter facing new challenges. Rising above her grief and loss to fulfill her mother's last wish, the author finds strength, surprising joy, and, finally, healing.

"A fully absorbing and inherently engaging read, 'Betty: A Memoir' is an extraordinary life story that is a riveting read from first page to last. Exceptionally well written, organized, and presented. By turns heartbreaking, empathy invoking, and ultimately inspiring..." - Midwest Book Review

Available on Amazon.com

To contact the authors:
marysteele444@gmail.com or ssteele1951@gmail.com

Made in United States
Cleveland, OH
22 March 2025